I0458691

PREPARE TO SURVIVE & THRIVE

PROJECTS TO LIVE OFF GRID WITH SUFFICIENT FOOD, WATER, & ELECTRICITY

WADE HOLLIS

CONTENTS

Copyright © 2024 Wade Hollis. All rights reserved.

The content within this book may not be reproduced, duplicated, or transmitted without direct written permission from the author or the publisher.

Under no circumstances will any blame or legal responsibility be held against the publisher or author for any damages, reparation, or monetary loss due to the information contained within this book, either directly or indirectly.

Legal Notice:

This book is copyright-protected. It is only for personal use. You cannot amend, distribute, sell, use, quote, or paraphrase any part of the content within this book without the consent of the author or publisher.

Disclaimer Notice:

Please note the information contained within this document is for educational and entertainment purposes only. All effort has been expended to present accurate, up-to-date, reliable, and complete information. No warranties of any kind are declared or implied. Readers acknowledge that the author is not engaged in the rendering of legal, financial, medical, or professional advice. The content within this book has been derived from various sources. Please consult a licensed professional before attempting any techniques outlined in this book.

By reading this document, the reader agrees that under no circumstances is the author responsible for any losses, direct or indirect, that are incurred as a result of the use of the information contained within this document, including, but not limited to, errors, omissions, or inaccuracies.

 Created with Vellum

INTRODUCTION

In a world where uncertainty is the only certainty, preparedness is not just an option; it's a necessity. Life is chaotic. When chaos strikes, how ready are you to protect what matters most in your life?

In the past several years, I have found myself increasingly plagued with uncertainty. The world keeps getting stranger and more dangerous, what with pandemics, wars, and natural disasters. Sometimes, it even felt like the world was ending, which gave me a lot of pause. What did I know about surviving when our systems weren't working? Could I take care of my most basic needs if I didn't have societal structures that handled them for me?

I began to look for a resource that helped me gain the skills that I suddenly realized I lacked. I couldn't find one, however, not one that clearly listed all the practical knowledge and step-by-step information that I needed to have in order to feel secure.

If you've picked up this book, you have probably experienced some of the same things that led me to write it in the first place. You want to know that when disaster strikes, you will be able to protect your family and your home and ensure that they remain safe and secure no matter what chaos reigns outside your four walls. You want to know that you won't go hungry just because grocery stores aren't open, that you won't go thirsty if running water stops working. You want to know that you can keep this protection in place as long as it's needed—not run out of supplies too early, leaving you at the mercy of whatever problem is taking place in the broader world.

I wanted to know all these things, too, but my research revealed that finding a guide that contained all I needed to know wasn't available. I knew I couldn't be alone in wanting this information, so I developed my own framework to aggregate this information, why it matters, and the various steps and shortcuts I've learned along the way that will help you turn information into action.

The result was the OUTLAST framework, which will guide the chapters of this book. Through this framework, you will learn how to:

- O: Optimize Your Shelter
- U: Use Every Drop
- T: Take Charge of Your Food Supply
- L: Leverage Your Livestock and Food Stock
- A: Amp Up Your Energy Independence
- S: Stay Safe
- T: Transcend Survival

This book will be your guide through preparing yourself for life off the grid, something that, though we all hope won't come to pass, seems like an increasingly dangerous possibility in the alarming, fast-paced modern world we live in. With this step-by-step manual, you will be able to build a robust survival plan that keeps your family safe, no matter what the world throws at you—and you'll have all the resources in one place so that they're ready whenever you need them.

With this book, you can reshape how you interact with the world. For me, I no longer view the grocery store as a painful reminder of how modern convenience has made me helpless in the face of true disaster. Instead, I see it as a handy place to pick up snacks—but not a place whose existence I rely upon. Allow me to assure you, it's a much more comfortable place to be—though you'll soon be able to see for yourself.

Let's get to work so that any disaster that strikes—whether it be natural or man-made—becomes something you can weather and any new version of the world a place where you can thrive.

1

CHAPTER ONE—AHEAD OF THE CURVE: WHY YOU NEED A GAME PLAN NOW

"The time to repair the roof is when the sun is shining."

— PRESIDENT JOHN F. KENNEDY

Day to day life is hectic, which can make thinking about "someday" challenging. The problem with putting off preparation for "someday," is that it could come tomorrow, next month, next year...or never. But you don't know—not until it arrives.

However, disasters are more common than we think. The American Red Cross notes, for example, that people in Kentucky are at "high risk" of landslides, earthquakes, tornadoes, hurricanes, floods, home fires, extreme heat, thunderstorms, winter storms, and power outages—and that's just one state. All of these beg the question: Do you know all the common disasters in your area? And are you prepared for all of them?

In this chapter, we'll discuss different kinds of disasters, from natural calamities to societal breakdown, so that you know the potential effects of the dangers that could strike your area, how to prepare for the worst, and what to do when trouble inevitably arrives at your door.

WHAT'S THE WORST THAT COULD HAPPEN?

Whenever I hear this question, I wince—because most people ask it as a flippant excuse for why they haven't prepared for disasters, not as an actual test to check that their preparations are sufficient. The more I learned about preparing for survival off-grid, the more I have embraced the idea that this is not a rhetorical question. It's one that really needs to be answered for each scenario you could potentially face.

Earthquakes

Earthquakes occur when shifts in the Earth's tectonic plates cause the ground to shift and tremble, usually across large areas. Earthquakes can cause tsunamis, landslides, avalanches, fires, and building collapse. Earthquakes can happen anywhere at any time, though they are most common in places that lie along fault lines or places where tectonic plates meet. In the United States, this includes Alaska, California, Hawaii, Oregon, Washington State, and the Mississippi River Valley (Ready "Earthquakes" 2024).

Hurricanes

Hurricanes are large storm systems that begin over water and move toward land. Hurricanes can cause high winds and heavy rain. Storm surges that lead to rapid rises in water levels are the leading cause of hurricane-related fatalities in the U.S. (Ready "Hurricanes" 2024). Wind damage (including tornadoes), rip currents, and flooding can cause property damage or injury. Hurricanes take place along the U.S. coastline; hurricane season generally runs from June 1-November 30, though the California coast may see hurricanes earlier in May (Ready "Hurricanes" 2024).

Explosion

Responding to explosions can be challenging, as their cause is often unclear. If an explosion occurs in your area, be cautious that a secondary explosion may happen or that other secondary threats may be in play (for example, if the explosion is due to drug manufacture, hazardous chemicals may be in the air, while natural gas explosions can lead to physical threats like broken glass or debris). Explosions are not common in the United States, but when they do occur, they are most frequently caused by gas leaks (Haupt and Young 2022). If you smell gas in your home, evacuate immediately.

Fire

The American Red Cross cautions that once a fire begins in your home, you may have a mere two minutes to escape before facing dangerous burns, smoke inhalation, or death (American Red Cross "Home Fire Safety" n.d.). Fires can also lead to property damage, including the loss of your home. Fires commonly start due to unsafe cooking practices and the use of portable space heaters, fireplaces, or wood stoves (Haupt and Young 2022).

Floods

Flooding, or the overflow of water onto land that is normally dry, happens due to heavy rains, when dams break, or when snow melts quickly. Flooding can cause damage with only a few inches, though it can, in more serious cases, cover a house to its rooftop. Floods are the most common weather-related natural disaster and occur across the United States (NOAA National Severe Storms Laboratory "Flooding Basics" n.d.).

Flash floods are the most dangerous kind of flooding, as they move quickly, sometimes causing extreme rises in water levels in only minutes. This limits reaction time. Densely populated areas, such as cities, are at higher risk for flash floods, as construction and pavement reduce the area where water can be absorbed by the ground. Mountains and steep hills can also lead to rapid runoff, which leads to flash flooding.

Terrorist Attack

As a man-made disaster, terrorist attacks are unpredictable. They can cause significant casualties or damage to infrastructure. They may involve biological agents that can kill or disable humans, livestock, and crops (Ready "Biohazard Exposure" 2023). These may be spread via physical contact, the air, or food and drink. Terrorist attacks can also incorporate cyber-attacks, which can lead to financial losses, the theft of personal information, or damage to institutions and governments (Ready 2022).

Severe Winter Weather

Severe winter weather includes extreme cold, hail, heavy snowfall, ice, and high winds. These conditions compromise transportation, heat, power, communication, and the availability of important supplies. Schools and workplaces may also be closed. Most deaths from winter storms are related to traffic incidents or exposure (NOAA National Severe Storms Laboratory "Winter Weather Basics" n.d.).

Wildfire

Wildfires are unplanned fires that burn in natural areas. Wildfires are commonly associated with forests but can also spread quickly across grasslands and prairies, causing devastation to ecosystems and communities. Recent years have shown wildfires growing larger, longer lasting, and more dangerous than ever before (American Red Cross "Wildfire Safety" n.d.).

Drought

Though every part of the United States sees periods of reduced rainfall, when these periods of abnormally dry weather persist long enough to cause shortages in the water supply, they become classified as droughts. Droughts can be meteorological (when an area gets less rain than is typical), agricultural (when there is insufficient moisture in the soil to meet crops' needs), socioeconomic (when water supply cannot meet human needs), and hydrological (when surface and underground water levels are below normal) [American Red Cross "Drought Preparedness" n.d.]. Local drought conditions may lead to water restrictions in your area.

Landslide

Landslides can occur following earthquakes, storms, wildfires, volcanic eruptions, or human land modifications. Landslides are most deadly when they occur rapidly. Signs of landslides include sudden rushing water or mud (either heard or seen), the sound of trees or rocks cracking together, or large boulders that indicate past debris flow. Wildfire burn areas are exceptionally susceptible to landslides for several years after the fire (Ready "Landslides & Debris Flow" 2024).

Pandemic

Pandemics, like the recent COVID-19 or Coronavirus pandemic, are typically caused by viruses, as these spread quickly from person to person and can span several countries and affect large quantities of people before being adequately detected (Ready "Pandemics" 2023). New viruses can appear anywhere and at any time. Novel pandemics often involve fast-paced discovery and new information, which means that taking more precautions rather than fewer can help prevent infection or death when a new illness is quickly spreading.

WHY IT PAYS TO BE PREPARED

Preparing *before* disaster strikes is often the difference between life and death. Some emergency preparation protocols can prevent crises from occurring in the first place or mitigate their effects when they do strike. Fireproofing your home, for example, means preventing the likelihood of fire sparking while allowing controlled burns in wildfire-prone areas can limit the destructive potential of a natural fire.

Even when dealing with disasters that cannot be entirely prevented or diminished, preparedness is key. Having predetermined escape or evacuation routes for natural disasters can spare you from being trapped in a damaged, unsafe building. Having food and water stored can protect you against dehydration or starvation if you become trapped in your home following an earthquake. Having and rehearsing emergency plans will promote a quick response when the emergency occurs, as this enables you to feel confident instead of confused. This practice can also reduce panic, both before and during the crisis. If you know how to respond, you are less likely to flounder in a key moment—which can make a bad situation worse.

NOT JUST DRILLS...PRACTICE DRILLS THAT COULD JUST SAVE YOUR LIFE

Having an emergency plan is little help if you are unable to enact it in a moment of need. To take your emergency preparedness from the hypothetical to the real, run regular drills with your family. Experts recommend that these drills be rehearsed every six months to ensure that they are fresh in your mind, no matter when a crisis hits (Oklahoma Department of Emergency Management 2024). Staggering drills so that you complete one every month or so can help you keep these on your calendar and keep the importance of running emergency drills fresh in your mind.

The drills below are designed for families, though the California Childcare Health Program notes that children may be more comfortable with emergency protocols if first introduced in a playful setting, such as using follow-the-leader to teach them to move in an orderly fashion or playing "turtle" to teach children to duck down and cover their heads (2016). Infants or toddlers may need special equipment to move or protect them in various emergencies, while family members with special needs may have similar accommodations. Practice each drill with the needed specifications, according to what your family requires.

Home Fire Escape Plan

To prepare for your home fire escape drill:

- Draw a map of your home that includes all doors and windows.
- Ensure that each room has at least two points of escape.
- Ensure that doors and windows are not blocked.
- Choose an outside meeting place.

Once these elements have been identified, practice leaving the house quickly and efficiently and assembling it in your meeting space. Aim to have all family members outside in two minutes or less; you can signal the start of your drill by pressing the test button on your fire alarm, which will associate the real sound of the alarm with the actions you perform in the drill. Ensure that family members can get out using alternate routes by indicating certain points of egress as "blocked" by fire.

Fires in apartment buildings and condominiums are particularly dangerous, as routes of escape are often less clear (U.S. Fire Administration n.d.). If you live in an apartment or condo, make sure that your drill involves closing your apartment door, does not rely on an elevator, and includes a stop to pull the fire alarm, though this last step should only be performed in the event of a true fire.

Tornado Preparedness Plan

The first step in your tornado preparedness plan is understanding the difference between a tornado watch, which means that you should be prepared as weather conditions may rapidly turn, and a tornado warning, which means it is time to act (US Department of Commerce "Understanding Tornado Alerts" n.d). The most severe alert is a tornado emergency, which means you need to find shelter immediately.

For your tornado preparedness plan, practice what to do when you are at home or away, including outside. For home drills, practice going to the basement or other interior rooms, staying away from windows, and covering your head. If you are away from home, such as at school or in the workplace, go to a designated tornado shelter location if one is available. If there is no designated location, avoid windows and large, open rooms—like cafeterias or gymnasiums.

For outside drills, practice finding a study shelter as quickly as possible. Advise your family that sheds and storage facilities are not sturdy enough to provide safety. The National Weather Service recommends driving to the closest shelter if you are in your vehicle when a tornado hits (US Department of Commerce "What to Do

During a Tornado" n.d.). Identify suitable shelters along your common routes (such as to and from work or school). For instances where you cannot seek shelter in time, practice getting low in your car and covering your head or finding a low-lying ditch or ravine where you can seek shelter.

Hurricane Preparedness Plan

Have two plans in action in advance of hurricanes: one for if you need to evacuate, one for if you need to shelter safely.

If you plan to evacuate:

- Know where you will go.
- Know what route you will take to get there. Do not rely on electronic navigation systems such as GPS devices or cell phones, as these may not have a signal during a weather emergency. Know that members of your family can get to your evacuation point using paper maps.
- Know where you will stay. If you plan to stay in a hotel or other paid lodging, budget accordingly. If you plan to stay with family members or friends, discuss your plan with them.

If you plan to shelter safely:

- Prepare your family and your home to be without power, gas, phone, water, or internet for extended periods. This includes having batteries for flashlights or lanterns, having stored potable water, and having food that can be prepared without heat and can last for a long time (such as canned beans, dried fruit or meat, or emergency rations).
- Identify and practice quickly accessing a designated safe shelter for periods of high winds. Seek an interior, windowless room that is on the lowest level that is safe from flooding.

- If flooding is common in your area, designate a higher-ground location where you can gather during flooding and practice getting there quickly.

Earthquake Drill

To conduct an earthquake drill with your family:

- Set a signal to indicate the start of the drill. If you choose to participate in regional ShakeOut (earthquake preparedness drills organized by organizations including the American Red Cross and FEMA), listen for the drill broadcast on the appointed date and time.
- During the drill, drop to the ground, take cover by getting under a sturdy table or other piece of furniture, and hold on until the shaking stops (indicated by the drill broadcast). If doing a self-timed drill, ensure that you hold your position for at least one minute. Remind your family that it is not safe to move during an earthquake.
- Once the simulated earthquake period is over, examine your home for things that could have fallen and injured someone. Move those items to a lower place or secure them to walls.
- Identify an evacuation plan and meeting point if your home is compromised by the earthquake. Ensure that each family member can get there, even if separated.
- Practice accessing supplies that you will need if you must shelter in place following an earthquake, including food, water, and first aid kits.

MAKING A 72-HOUR SURVIVAL KIT

Many of the drills discussed above depend on having adequate supplies to shelter in your home for an extended period. Experts recommend stocking a kit that allows for 72 hours of survival in your home. This kit should include:

Food and water:

- A minimum of one gallon of water per person per day. (For example, a family of four planning for three days should have twelve gallons of water safely stored.)
- Food that doesn't require cooking and won't spoil. Examples include granola, protein bars, trail mix, dried fruit, canned beans or fish (such as tuna), nuts, or powdered milk. Ensure that you have stocked enough food for your whole family for three days. Replace food annually.
- Pet food and water, if applicable.
- Infant formula or baby food, if applicable. Replace semi-annually.

First aid and medical needs:

- General first aid supplies including bandages (include both adhesive bandages and larger wrap-style bandages), antiseptic wipes, antibacterial wipes, gauze, instant hot and cold packs, tweezers, scissors, isopropyl alcohol, hand sanitizer.
- Prescription medications. Check these semi-annually to ensure they have not expired.
- Over-the-counter medications such as pain relievers, allergy medication, antacids, anti-diarrhea medications, and laxatives. Check these semi-annually to ensure they have not expired.
- Sanitation and anti-contagion protection, including face masks (to avoid spreading germs or inhaling dust), moist towelettes, and sterile gloves.
- Extra prescription glasses or contact lenses, if applicable.

Toiletries:

- Toilet paper.
- Feminine supplies.
- Diapers (if applicable).
- Extra clothing. Check sizes annually for families with children.

Equipment:

- Flashlights and batteries
- Pocket knife and multi-tool
- Hand-operated can opener
- Waterproof matches
- Cash in small bills and prepaid phone cards
- Wrench or pliers
- Battery-powered or hand-crank radio
- Cell phone with charger and extra pre-charged battery
- Local maps
- Eating utensils
- Garbage bags for sanitary disposal
- Whistles or flares
- Duct tape
- Warm clothes and bedding
- Copies of personal documents, including emergency contacts
- Extra sets of house and car keys

Store your equipment in a waterproof container, preferable with wheels, in a place in your house that is easy to access. If you have children, consider including entertainment items, such as toys or puzzles.

MENTALLY PREPARING FOR A DISASTER

While physical preparations for disasters are important, they do not necessarily help prepare emotionally for the chaos of a true emergency. The Canadian Red Cross notes that over 80 percent of people recover from disasters without prolonged distress (n.d.). To help anticipate your emotional reaction to disasters, consider anticipating how you think you will react to stress and naming how you think you will feel. Then, identify solutions to manage that stress when it arises. Though these steps may seem secondary to other preparations, having a network of support already in place in advance of a crisis means that you will have somewhere to turn when you are facing the reality of a natural disaster, manmade attack, or health crisis.

This chapter has addressed the basics of preparing for disasters that inevitably come in life. Many people will stop here and consider themselves ready for whatever life throws their way. If you found yourself wondering, however, what happens if a disaster lasts longer than the 72 hours covered by your supplies, continue to our next chapter, where we will discuss how to make your home livable and safe even during a long-term crisis.

2

CHAPTER TWO—O: OPTIMIZE YOUR SHELTER

B uilding a shelter is easier said than done. Even if you're an avid outdoorsman, you may be surprised to learn that there are stark differences between pitching a tent in good weather and setting up shelter in a survival situation (Montana 2015). In this chapter, we'll discuss how to build a successful, optimized shelter—so you don't end up trying to stay safe in an improperly secured, cold shelter that is open to the elements. Or worse, you don't want to find yourself stuck in a "man trap," a shelter that collapses in on you while you're inside, risking injury or death.

SHOULD YOU STAY OR SHOULD YOU GO?

The first consideration when building a shelter comes before you begin to construct anything at all. While some disasters are best survived by staying where you are, others may require evacuation. When deciding whether to stay or go, consider the following:

- Is your area or home vulnerable? Mobile homes or RVs are not safe during most natural disasters, nor are areas that flood frequently. If your house is previously damaged or otherwise in need of repair, you cannot safely ride out a storm at home ("Evacuate or Stay" 2020).

- Is there an immediate threat to your life if you remain behind? Reasons may include extreme flash flooding or wildfire.
- Have you been ordered by officials to evacuate?
- Is it safe to evacuate? If evacuation routes are compromised, you may need to shelter in place to optimize your safety (City of Vancouver n.d.).

SHELTERING IN PLACE

Sheltering in place, or going and staying inside the nearest safe building, is a common safety strategy when disaster strikes. Develop plans with your family for sheltering in place at home, school, and other common locations, though understand that you can practice shelter-in-place procedures anywhere—and may need to, as disasters can strike at unpredictable times.

The basics of shelter-in-place are simple. Find a safe, sturdy location (not including sheds, temporary buildings, or mobile homes), go inside, and stay in a room as far from windows and doors as possible. Then, wait in your shelter until the danger has passed. The Centers for Disease Control advise using your phone as little as possible while sheltering in place, so to keep lines open for emergency responders ("Stay Put" 2017).

If you are sheltering in place in response to a chemical hazard, lock all your doors and windows and turn off air conditioners, fans, or other devices that encourage air to come in from outside. Seal windows using duct tape and plastic and avoid drinking tap water, which may be contaminated (FEMA 2021).

If sheltering in place after flooding, either because you were instructed by officials not to evacuate or the disaster progressed too quickly for evacuation, avoid rooms that have no egress, such as basements or closed attics. Instead, go to the highest level of the building. If necessary, go onto the roof to avoid rising waters (FEMA 2021).

If sheltering in place after a nuclear detonation, go to the basement or lowest level of a structure. Brick and concrete walls will best protect from radioactive fallout, which begins to accumulate about ten minutes following an explosion (FEMA 2021). If you were outside after the fallout arrived, remove your outer clothing and keep it away from humans and animals. Wash exposed skin and hair if possible.

Most shelter-in-place orders last only a few hours. Do not try to retrieve your children from school; they will be sheltered in place there according to school protocols, and trying to retrieve them during the shelter-in-place order will put you at greater risk (CADPH 2017).

When sheltering in place, consider these tips (OLLU n.d.):

- You can further secure your shelter-in-place location by locking or barricading the door.
- In certain circumstances (such as active shooter situations), you should avoid attracting attention. Do so by closing the shades, turning off lights, and silencing your cell phone.
- If you are outside and cannot locate a safe building to shelter-in-place, use benches, trees, or dumpsters as protection from hazards.
- If you are in an unfamiliar place when a shelter-in-place order commences, consider bathrooms or closets to hide, as these rarely have windows and are often far from the building's outer walls.

SEEKING SHELTER SOMEPLACE ELSE

Depending on the emergency and your circumstances when it strikes, you may be unable to seek shelter in an existing building. In this case, you will need to build yourself an emergency survival shelter. Shelter is a core physiological need and one that is less portable in most situations than food or water (Truchon 2023). That means that when disaster strikes, you will need a "home base" shelter to help guard you from predators, pests, and the elements while you determine your next steps.

Let's look at different types of survival shelters that you can build, discuss how to construct them, and identify which shelters are most appropriate for various situations.

Round Lodge

Round lodges have a conical shape like tipis, a solid doorway, and, typically, a smoke hole in the top. Round lodges survive in wet climates (they were used in pre-Roman Britain) and can be thatched with grass or leaf litter (MacWelch 2019). Round lodges can offer protection for multiple people and can last for extended periods of time. To build a round lodge (Positive Adventures 2020):

1. Gather approximately a dozen tall, sturdy branches. Seek the straightest branches you can find.

2. Lean the branches together, moving in a clockwise direction. These should come together in a cone shape. Leave an opening to enter and exit, ideally placed away from the direction of the wind.

3. Lash the branches together at the top to keep your cone in place.

4. Fill in walls with vegetation to increase insulation, leaving a hole at the top for ventilation.

If you have a tarp, you can make a tarp tipi, a simpler (and often smaller) version of this shelter. To build a tarp tipi, lean the branches together as you would make a round lodge. Aim to build your framework so that your tarp can cover it completely. Wrap the tarp around the branches, securing at the top with a rope. Tie down the tarp, leaving a door flap to be closed for protection from the elements or opened for ventilation (MacWelch 2019).

Ramada

Ramadas have flat roofs and open walls that provide shade in hot, dry environments without blocking cooling breezes. Ramadas are constructed from beams, at least four upright posts, and roofing (Positive Adventures 2020). Note that the ramada's flat roof makes it poor at blocking rain; heavy rainfall may damage your shelter. To build a ramada (Emergency Essentials 2017):

1. Seek sturdy branches to make your posts (seek four for smaller ramadas or more for larger structures). Sink these into the ground by digging a hole, lowering the post inside, then refilling and tamping down the dirt.

2. Find lightweight support beams. Fasten these between your posts to create a steady structure.

3. Layer the roof with a brush or a tarp to provide shade.

4. (Optional) Use a tarp or other material to create removable walls to help trap heat after the sun goes down.

If you have a tarp, you can make a tarp wing variation on this structure by tying opposing corners to posts or trees. For a tarp wing, put two opposing corners higher and two lower. Unlike a ramada, this sloped structure will keep off rain as well as sun (MacWelch 2019).

Quinzhee

A quinzhee is a cold-weather shelter that, though shaped like an igloo, is much simpler to construct. This shelter relies on packed snowfall to protect you from the elements. Unlike snow caves, which can collapse if built with the wrong kind of snow, quinzhees can be built with almost all types of snowfall (Emergency Essentials 2017). To construct your quinzhee (MacWelch 2019):

1. Pile some moveable gear (such as a backpack) under a tarp.

2. Pile snow over the tarp and gear, packing it down and adding more until it is approximately two feet thick all the way around.

3. Insert twelve-inch-long sticks around the dome. Seek to add forty to fifty of these guide sticks into the dome's exterior.

4. Burrow into the side of the dome to retrieve your tarp and gear.

5. Excavate snow from the inside of the mound until you reach

the base of each guide stick. This will ensure the dome is uniformly thick (with about one foot of snow on all sides).

6. Make a ventilation hole about the size of your fist in the roof of the quinzhee.

Snow Cave

Though quinzhees are more reliable in areas with no vegetation and little to moderate amounts of snow, a snow cave may be your only option in areas with very deep snow (Emergency Essentials 2017). To build a snow cave (MacWelch 2019):

1. Select a snow back with deep, solid snow.

2. Dig into the side, seeking a low spot called a "cold well," or a place where the colder air can fall and collect.

3. Next, into the back of your cold well, dig up and over to create a sleeping platform. This should be the highest part of the shelter.

4. Dig a hole through the roof of the shelter that is at least six inches in diameter. The distance between the ceiling of your sleeping platform and the external snowbank should be at least two feet thick so that the snow does not collapse when you make this hole. If the snow is still falling outside, regularly check to ensure this hole has not become blocked.

5. (Optional) Block the front of your cave with a backpack or chunk of snow to keep out more cold air. If you take this step, it becomes even more important to ensure that your ventilation hole is open.

Lean-To

A lean-to is useful in its versatility, as it can be built out of many common natural materials. To make a lean-to (Emergency Essentials 2017):

1. Wedge a sturdy pole between two trees.

2. Layer one side of the pole with branches.

3. Cover branches with leaf litter or other vegetation.

4. (Optional) Add a second side to the lean-to to provide extra protection if the wind changes direction.

If you cover a two-sided lean-to with leaf litter and pile more leaves inside for bedding, you have a leaf hut, which provides more insulation than a simple lean-to (MacWelch 2019).

Simple Tarp Shelters

A tarp is one of the most versatile items when it comes to providing shelter. Though a tarp cn its own (or with very few amendments) may not provide as much protection as more robust shelters, it can be used in several ways to keep you out of the elements.

Wedge Tarp

A simple wedge tarp shelter works best in windy conditions when the wind is coming from a consistent direction. To build, stake two corners (but not opposing corners) into the wind. Tie a line up the center of the tarp, then tie the remaining two corners down sharply (MacWelch 2019). If you put large rocks or logs under the first corners, the edges of the tarp wil: also collect rainwater.

A-Frame Tarp Shelter

This structure is like a wedge tarp shelter, though it provides less protection from the elements and more ventilation. To build this shelter, suspend rope between two trees. Lay the tarp across this cord, then lash down all four corners.

Tarp Burrito

This no-frills shelter gets set up quickly and can protect you from the worst dampness of the night. However, there is a tradeoff to the simplicity: the tarp burrito has little ventilation, which means that dew and frost will accumulate overnight in all but the driest conditions (MacWelch 2019). To build your tarp burrito, lay down your tarp, then fold over one side about a third of the way. Then, fold again in the same direction, making a roll shape with the seam underneath. Tuck one end underneath the roll to close it off. Your sleeping bag can be shoved in the other end.

Desert Tarp

The double roof layer of this shelter helps keep heat off you. To build it, take two tarps and lash them to low supports with about one foot of air space between them. If your tarp is larger, you can fold it in half to create the same effect (MacWelch 2019). Tie your stakes to four anchors. Keep this structure low to the ground to maximize its cooling potential.

Tarp Hammock

When the ground is wet or crawling with pests, getting off the ground is a priority. To improvise this hammock, you will need a tarp and rope. Roll the long side of your tarp and roll it inward to the halfway point. Repeat on the other side until you have a long, two-roll bundle. On each end of the bundle, tie a "sheet bend," which involves wrapping rope around the end of your bundle, folding the end over that wrap, and then tying rope around the folded portion. Securely tie your hammock to two trees, reaching as high as you can, as the hammock will settle with your weight as the knots cinch (MacWelch 2019).

PREPARING YOUR SHELTER-BUILDING KIT

While many of the shelters discussed above can be built primarily out of things provided by nature, having a few manmade tools can ensure that you have more options in a survival setting and maximize your comfort and safety in extreme conditions.

To best prepare yourself for building survival shelters when the need arises, prepare a shelter-building kit that contains essentials. Take this kit with you whenever you go into wilderness settings or when evacuating your home during an emergency.

Your shelter-building kit should include (Truchon 2023):

- A backpack or rucksack that you can easily carry. Moving through difficult terrains is much easier when your hands are free instead of occupied carrying your equipment. Choose a backpack that is large enough to hold all your essentials but not too heavy for you to carry over long distances.

- Lights. Consider packing both a handheld flashlight, which you can point easily wherever you need light, and a headlamp, which allows for hands-free illumination. Ensure that you have batteries for your light source and consider hand-crank or solar-powered options to avoid relying on battery power.

- Tarps. As we've referenced, tarps are one of the most versatile tools for building shelters. If possible, pack at least two—one for keeping you off the ground and one for sheltering you from rain and wind.

- Cordage. Most structures require some form of lashing, which necessitates cordage. Many survival experts prefer synthetic paracord, which is lightweight and strong, as it was initially developed for military use (Emergency Prep Gear n.d.).

- A knife. Knives are versatile survival tools, as they will let you strip branches, cut cordage, make other tools, or defend yourself.

- Firestarter. A fire can mean the difference between life and death in cold climates. While lighters can run out of fluid, fire starters make sparks without any extra fuel.

- First aid kit. Though this is not technically an element of shelter-building, survival situations often lead to minor injuries. Having a first aid kit will keep those injuries from becoming more painful or dangerous.

- (Optional) Handheld ax. Having a small, portable ax can help when cutting thicker branches to build stronger, more durable shelters.

- (Optional) Sleeping bag or bed roll. Though some wilderness scenarios will have leaf litter, which can make a comfortable sleeping platform, having a sleeping bag or bed roll can make your nights more comfortable, which can leave you better rested and, therefore, more prepared to tackle survival tasks. In frigid environments, a sleeping bag becomes more than comfort, as its warmth can protect you during the coldest parts of the day when you are moving the least and therefore generating the least warmth on your own.

While seeking food and water might seem like the most obvious first step in survival, you can go several days without water and several weeks without food. You won't, however, be able to secure those necessary elements if you freeze overnight or are harmed by predators. Shelter is, therefore, the first and most crucial thing to establish in any off-grid survival situation.

Now that we've discussed how to build a safe, protective shelter in various environments, we can turn to other important needs. In our next chapter, we'll look at unlocking hydration so that you can ensure that you have sufficient water to last you through any disaster, even protracted ones.

3

CHAPTER THREE—U: USE EVERY DROP

Consider the rule of three: Humans can, on average, last three minutes without oxygen, three days without water, and three weeks without food (Svalbarði n.d.). This means that, in most survival situations, finding water should be your priority after securing your shelter.

This, as with most aspects of surviving off the grid, can be easier said than done. When you are seeking water under the threat of dehydration—which can cause your body to shut down and your organs to fail—you need water that is potable and consistently accessible (Beall 2020). Terrain can work against you when it comes to accessing this water, as expedition guide Chaz Powell learned when he suffered from dehydration even when the Zambezi River was in his eyeline—but down an inaccessible gorge at a drop of several hundred feet (Beall 2020).

Though Powell ultimately survived by making the risky climb down to the river while he waited for rescue, he reports experiencing the effects of severe dehydration. Without adequate water, your body cannot regulate blood temperature, experiences severe drops in blood pressure, and struggles with mental processes. If you still don't get the water you need, you risk organ failure, starting with your kidneys (Johnson 2024). These complications make it increasingly difficult to access water, which, in turn, makes survival less likely.

In this chapter, we will discuss all the crucial elements of securing a water source in survival settings, including finding water, purifying it, and recycling it.

SOURCING YOUR WATER

Not all water sources are equally beneficial, and when we've spent years relying on clean water coming from every faucet, it can be challenging to source this key survival necessity. When living off the grid, water sources have different pros and cons.

Well Water

Well drilling is a common way to get a reliable water source off-grid. When properly drilled and maintained, wells provide a consistent source of fresh, usually drinkable, water. Sourcing well water requires advanced preparation; drilling an 150-foot well in the United States costs an average of $5,500 and necessitates considering environmental impacts before digging (Bradshaw 2023).

Natural Off-Grid Water Sources

Naturally occurring water sources are ideal for off-grid survival in that they are preexisting, recurrent sources of water. Different water sources will, however, require different levels of treatment to be usable. When seeking natural sources for drinking water, privilege running water over still water. Make natural springs your first choice, as they arise directly from underground sources, making them least likely to have contaminants (Bradshaw 2023). Collect water directly from the spring to store for drinking.

If a spring is unavailable, choose other running water sources next, such as rivers or streams. Flowing water is typically abundant, though the cleanliness can vary; this water may be polluted by agricultural or industrial runoff (Bradshaw 2023). Water from streams or rivers should be filtered and disinfected before being consumed or used for washing.

Lakes and ponds should be your third-tier choice for sourcing natural water. While lakes and ponds provide steady sources of water, they can contain pollutants and contaminants in varying concentrations, particularly because the water is unmoving (Bradshaw 2023). To ensure that lake or pond water is drinkable, you must remove sediment by letting it settle to the bottom of harvested water, then filter and disinfect the harvested water.

RAINWATER HARVESTING

Rainwater, depending on your climate, can also provide a reliable source of water that is low in contaminants. Rainwater is also better for plants and gardens than tap water in many places, as on-grid water is often treated with chlorine ("Rainwater Harvesting 101" 2024).

One of the most common ways to collect rainwater is by letting it run off your roof, as this is an impermeable and often sloped surface that lends itself to collecting falling precipitation. To assess how much rainwater you can collect, first, know the square footage of your roof. U.S. Census data cites the average roof size at 1,700 square feet, though smaller houses will have as low as 1,000 square feet and larger houses as much as 3,000 (Tarver 2020).

From there, you can calculate your collection potential using the following formula ("Rainwater Harvesting 101" 2024):

1 in. of rain x 1 sq. ft.= 0.623 gallons

This means that the small estimated roof (1,000 sq. ft.) can provide 623 gallons of rainwater with one inch of rainfall, while the average roof (1,700 sq. ft.) can provide about 1,060 gallons with one inch of rainfall.

Estimating the viability of rainwater harvesting for your water needs depends on your climate. In 2023, for example, Connecticut saw 61.18 inches of rainfall, well above the national average, which is around thirty inches per year for the contiguous states (Statista 2023). New Mexico was the driest state that year; it received only 10.86 inches of rainfall. Statistics indicate that rainfall is trending upward in the United States in the twenty-first century compared to the twentieth (Statista 2023).

If rainwater harvesting is viable in your climate, consider some of the following strategies for collecting rainwater.

Rain Barrels

Rain barrels are the simplest and most common system for collecting rainwater. To implement this system, simply put a barrel under a gutter downspout to collect rainwater. Pros to this system include the ease of installation, the readiness of materials, and size constraints—barrels are small and portable and therefore can fit into almost any space. Cons come from capacity issues; most rain barrels hold only about 50 to 100 gallons, which means you can lose collection opportunities if they overflow ("Rain Harvesting 101" 2024).

Dry System

This larger-scale version of a rain barrel gets its name from the collection pipe, which dries after each rainfall. To build a "dry system" rainfall collector, you install a large, enclosed tank next to your house, then connect your gutter system to the top of the tank so that water empties inside your container (Wateroam 2024).

This system can capture and store large amounts of water, which makes it ideal for climates that have infrequent large storms, rather than consistent moderate rainfall ("Rain Harvesting 101" 2024). Because your gutter pipe will connect directly to the tank, the tank must be located directly next to your house, which can create space issues.

Wet System

The most complex but most productive method of rainwater collection is called a "wet system" because, unlike in the "dry system," its underground pipes do not empty. This system connects a large water collection tank to multiple gutters and downspouts using underground pipes. As rain falls, the rainwater fills the underground piping, which then raises the water in the vertical pipes until it enters the tank ("Rainwater Harvesting 101" 2024). For this pressure-based system to work, the tank inlet must be lower than the lowest gutter on your house, and all piping must have watertight connections.

Pros of this system include the ability to harvest water from your entire collection surface, not just one gutter spout on your roof. The tank can also be located away from your house, which can improve space considerations. A wet system, is, however, more expensive and complicated to implement than the other systems.

Designing a DIY Rainwater Harvesting System

You can begin rainwater harvesting with a simple system you can build at home, often in the afternoon or over the weekend. To create a simple homemade rain barrel system (Sakawsky 2019):

1. Choose a suitable location. Find a corner of your house that already has a drainpipe and that has space for your barrel and stand.

2. Build a stand. This step is optional, as you can put barrels directly on the ground, but adding a stand allows you to put a spigot at the bottom of the barrel, which makes retrieval easier (and helps prevent dislodging your system by regularly removing the lid). You can build a stand from scrap wood, cinderblocks, bricks, or anything sturdy enough to hold about 300 pounds of water. Ensure that it is level so that your barrel doesn't wobble or tip over.

3. Choose your barrels. While barrels specifically for rainwater collection are commercially available, you can make your own more affordable option from plastic garbage cans.

4. Route your drainpipe to your barrel. You can do this via elbows that match your extant piping or a flexible drainpipe. If you are using the DIY trash can barrels, trace the drainpipe top and cut a hole in the lid.

5. (Optional) Add spigots. Cut a hole in the bottom of the barrel; a 3/4 inch hole accommodates most spigots. Insert the spigot, then seal with silicone or rubber washers.

6. (Optional) Add overflow drain. Cut a hole near the top of the

barrel and insert another spigot (left open) or pipe. This will prevent any overflow from spilling over the side of your barrel and potentially dislodging the lid. Optionally, you can connect the overflow pipe to another collection apparatus to ensure the collected water doesn't go to waste. To implement this overflow collection, route your pipe to the new barrel (as in Step 4) and proceed through the remainder of the steps for the secondary barrel.

7. Add a debris screen. This will prevent leaves and water-breeding bugs like mosquitos from getting into your water supply. To implement this, put window screen material (cut slightly larger than the diameter of your barrel) atop the barrel opening. If your barrel has a lid, you can use that to secure the screen material. If not, staple it securely in place.

8. (Optional) Secure the rain barrel either to the side of your house or to the stand. This will prevent it from tipping over when it is insufficiently full.

9. Apply the lid and put a rerouted drainpipe through the hole.

Rain barrels are easy to implement but require regular maintenance. Clean your barrels about once per year using a three percent bleach solution. Empty your rain barrels before freezing temperatures hit your area so that the water doesn't freeze and crack your containment system (Rea 2021). Barrels can take several hours to empty when full, so plan where your water can be used in advance of a freeze—so that you can use the water rather than waste it when you need to drain it rapidly. Apply a lid or store barrels upside down in winter to protect snow and debris from getting inside.

FILTERING AND PURIFYING YOUR WATER

Water that comes from the tap is filtered and purified long before it comes out of your faucet. When collecting your own water, whether from rain, wells, or natural sources, you need to filter and purify water yourself to make it potable.

There are several types of home water filters you can install to make your collected off-grid water suitable for household use (Hamilton 2023):

- **Sediment filtration:** Sediment filtration removes particles like rust, silt, or heavy metals. These filters are made from polypropylene or pleated polyester, and the micron rating indicates its filtration strength. The U.S. National Park Service notes that filtrations systems with absolute pore sizes one micron filter or less can also remove parasites like giardia and cryptosporidium, which may be especially important when sourcing from lakes or rivers (NPS n.d.).
- **Activated Carbon Block (ACB) Filtration** or **Granular Activated Carbon (GAC) Filtration:** These filtration systems use fine carbon powder to remove chlorine taste, lead, and volatile organic compounds from your water. The ACB uses a block form of the carbon, held together by a binding agent, while the GAC system leaves carbon in its granular form. The GAC has a higher filtration rate.
- **Reverse Osmosis (RO) Filtration:** This system uses water pressure to force water through a semipermeable membrane that removes organic compounds. Note that this system filters slowly and requires a pressurized tank.
- **Ion Exchange (IX):** This system uses specialized resin that softens water and removes dissolved ions, metals, minerals, and acids. Note that this system does not remove organic contaminants and microorganisms.
- **Ultrafiltration (UF):** This system uses hydrostatic pressure to filter out parasites, bacteria, and viruses. UF membranes can only treat water with low concentrations of dissolved solids, so another filter must be used before undergoing the UF process.

After you filter solids out of your water, you will need to disinfect it to remove the remaining organisms in the water. To disinfect your water, try these methods:

- **Boiling**: Boiling is the simplest and most effective way to kill pathogens in your water (NPS n.d.). Elevation affects boiling times; if you are below 6,500 feet, bring water to a rolling boil for one minute before considering it drinkable. If you are above 6,500 feet, keep water at a rolling boil for three minutes. Cons to boiling water include the difficulty of scaling to accommodate large quantities and the wait time to let the water cool (unless you intend to use it for a hot beverage, such as coffee or tea).

- **Chemical Disinfection**: You can use water-disinfecting tablets or liquid drops, usually made from iodine or chlorine dioxide, to disinfect natural water. Follow instructions provided by the manufacturer but note that the time between application and disinfection may vary considerably. Some tablets may not be safe for people who are pregnant or have iodine sensitives (NPS n.d.). Note that disinfectants for potable water are different from other water disinfectant tablets—such as those designed to purify pool water, which cannot be used to make water drinkable.

- **UV Light Purifiers**: These battery-operated purifiers can be used to disinfect small quantities of clear water and need continuous use for a determined period to work (follow manufacturer's instructions). Larger ultraviolet disinfection systems can be installed at the household level (Hamilton 2023).

DIY Home Water Filtration System

While many water filtration systems are commercially available, you can also build a DIY version to make your system more affordable and to ensure you know how it works during a disaster. Ceramic water filters offer a durable option to filter water yourself.

To make a home water filtration system, you can use the two-bucket system. To best make this system, acquire (Gray and Bracken 2021):

- Two food-grade buckets with lids. Seek buckets that will easily stack.
- A ceramic water filter.
- A spigot.
- Siphon tubing that fits the bottom of your water filter.

To build the system:

1. Drill an air hole in the upper edge of the top bucket.

2. Drill a "starter hole" in the center of the bottom of the same bucket. Enlarge the hole with a larger bit.

3. Drill a hole of the same size to one of the lids.

4. Insert your ceramic filter into the bottom of the first bucket. The bottom of the filter will extend through the holes in both the bucket and the lid. Apply the washer and wing nut that came with the ceramic filter to the bottom of the lid. Tighten the wing nut and check for water leaks.

5. Add the siphon tube to the bottom of the filter, extending below the bucket and lid.

6. Drill a starter hole two inches below the bottom of the second bucket, then widen this hole to accommodate the spigot.

7. Attach the spigot with one washer on the outside and one on the inside.

8. Use the connecting lids to secure the bucket with the filter atop the bucket with the spigot. Add water to the top bucket to begin filtration, then apply the second lid to stop debris or further contaminants from getting into your water.

If you do not have access to a ceramic filter, you can create an emergency water filtration system by using natural filters (Wranglerstar 2023). To build this filter, drill ten smaller holes (instead of one large hole) in your upper bucket and lid, and replace the ceramic filter with layers of screening, clean sand, and gravel (about ½ inch pieces). Apply a third bucket on top, with ten holes drilled in, filled a third of the way with pulverized charcoal. Then, pour water so it trickles through the charcoal, then through the gravel and sand, and to the empty storage bucket. Filter the system several times to ensure clear water.

In an emergency, you can make a basic water filter with any two containers, pebbles, sand, and cloth (Cowan 2020). Gather the water in one container, then put cloth and pebbles across the second container and filter the water through the pebbles. Replace the pebbles with sand, then filter through the sand and cloth back to the first container. Repeat this process back to the second container with charcoal.

Homemade charcoal is better than charcoal briquettes, which may be treated with chemicals. You can make charcoal with any wood material. Darker wood will burn longer. To make the charcoal (City Prepping 2023):

1. Break the wood into small pieces. Pack the container as tightly as possible to prevent oxygen from igniting the wood.

2. Put the wood in a fire-resistant container such as an unlined paint can. Put a small hole in the lid of the can so that smoke can escape but excess oxygen can't get in (causing ignition).

3. Place the container in a robust campfire and stack burning material around it.

4. Leave containers in the fire until smoke stops coming out of the hole. Remove containers from the fire and let them cool completely before opening.

5. Store charcoal in an airtight container so it cannot absorb moisture from the air.

Disinfecting with the Sun

Once you've filtered your water so that it is free from particulates, you will need to disinfect it before it is potable.

Rays from the sun can provide a sustainable, effective, and low-cost method for disinfecting your water. Solar disinfection (SODIS) uses ultraviolet-A and infrared radiation, both part of solar radiation, to kill pathogens (CAWST n.d.). SODIS, unlike other applications, does not change the taste of the water. It is easily applicable at the household level, improves the microbiology quality of drinking water, and uses renewable energy (CTCN n.d.). SODIS is ranked as "highly effective" (compared to laboratory efficiency) at killing bacteria and giardia in water and "somewhat effective" at killing viruses and cryptosporidium (CAWST n.d.).

To build a solar disinfectant system at home, you will need (DeGunther 2016):

- An enclosure made of wood or sheet metal, built at an angle (with one side lower than the other
- A sheet of glass that covers the top of the enclosure
- Reflective material, such as aluminum foil
- Insulation
- Weather-resistant glue, such as silicon sealant
- Black paint
- Black tray that can absorb heat
- Catch trough for purified water
- Container to store purified water
- (Optional) Hinges

To build the SODIS system:

1. Paint the exterior of the enclosure black to increase heat absorption.

2. Glue insulation to the bottom of the enclosure.

3. Install the reflective material on the back and side walls of the enclosure.

4. Add a tray for contaminated water.

5. Place glass on top. Hinges can make it easier for this system to be opened and closed regularly.

6. Add a catch trough at the bottom of the glass. Angle it downward so that the purified water drains into your container.

7. Angle toward glass toward the sun.

This system will purify the water as it heats. The clean water will rise as condensation, which will then drain into your catch trough and storage container. Aim to get the water to at least 120 degrees Fahrenheit (or about 50 degrees Celsius) before drinking (CAWST n.d.).

Checking Water Potability

To evaluate water potability, start with clear signs that there is something amiss. If the water is cloudy or discolored, smells abnormal, or tastes strange, it is not ideal for drinking (Water Boy 2020). If your water leaves a white residue on surfaces, it likely has a high mineral content known as hard water, which can be detrimental to your health long term (DrinkPrime 2023). Consider investing in a Total Dissolved Solids (TDS) meter and pH testing kits to check if your water has excessive minerals or falls outside the recommended pH range (6.5-8.5; DrinkPrime 2023).

OFF-GRID PLUMBING SYSTEMS

Having a reliable plumbing system that works off the grid ensures your access to clean water and waste management even when disconnected from public utilities. For these systems, water conservation is essential, as you will be harvesting your water from natural sources, a well, or rainwater, all of which are more labor-intensive than accessing on-grid water.

The following systems will maximize your water use and keep your grey- and blackwater disposal sanitary:

- Greywater systems: A greywater system uses a three-valve system to hold your greywater (such as laundry or washing water) in a tank that recycles it and pumps it back into the land. Meanwhile, blackwater (which contains waste from the toilet) is pumped away from your home and crops. You can also reserve greywater manually and use it to water plants. Don't store greywater for more than twenty-four hours, or it may breed bacteria.

- Septic tanks: Septic tanks, already common in rural areas, hold wastewater outside your home while waste breaks down.
- Solar water heaters: These heaters use energy from the sun to heat your water, reducing the need for electricity.
- Low-flow toilets: These toilets minimize the water used per flush, leading to less blackwater waste.

Compost Toilets

Building a compost toilet can reduce blackwater waste entirely while providing a rich composting opportunity. To build this system, you will need the following (Gemeš 2024):

- Wood to build your toilet box
- Urine separator
- Toilet seat
- A long, narrow container for liquid waste
- Three 5-gallon buckets for solid waste
- Absorbents (such as sawdust, wood ash, or dried leaves)

To build the system:

1. Build your toilet box, considering a comfortable sitting height for members of your family. Make the box easy to open to remove waste containers.

2. Drill a hole in the top of the box that's the same size as your bucket for solid waste.

3. Add the toilet seat on top.

4. Install the urine separator on the front edge of the hole.

5. Install the liquid waste container beneath the urine separator and the solid waste container beneath the remainder of the hole.

6. Install a nearby container for absorbents. After you have used the toilet, you will scoop this on top of the solid waste to reduce odors.

When disposing of waste from compost toilets, ensure that you follow local guidelines so that waste does not seep into usable water sources. Clean the toilet with a water and vinegar mixture so that you do not compromise the compositing process.

With these strategies in play, you will never risk going those fatal three days without water at your disposal. With that need met, we will next look at tapping into nature's pantry to ensure that you have a consistent food supply, no matter how long you live off the grid.

4

CHAPTER FOUR—T: TAKE CHARGE OF YOUR FOOD SUPPLY

Hunger doesn't just affect your stomach. Instead, inadequate nutrition can affect our mood, which can make us struggle to make realistic decisions. Studies have also indicated that hunger can reduce cognitive performance by about fifteen percent (Frankel and Warren 2023).

These negative consequences of hunger can make survival situations much more deadly.

In this chapter, we'll discuss how to cultivate food sources for long-term self-sufficiency using methods including foraging and growing your own food. This will equip you with practical skills to identify, cultivate, and harvest sustainable food sources so that you know where your next meal is coming from, no matter the circumstances.

FORAGING FOR FOOD

When you need food quickly, you'll need to look for sources that already exist. In this section, we'll discuss how to forage, identify what is edible and what is not, and the basics of hunting and trapping.

Edible Plants

The plants that you pass by every day may be more nutritious than you think. When seeking something to eat that's already growing around you, look for:

- **Cattails:** These tall, reedy plants with distinctive red or brown cylinders at the top grow in large clumps near freshwater. Nearly all parts of the cattail plant are edible, and they can be found across the U.S. and Canada. Cattail roots can be eaten raw, though their taste may improve when boiled. The stems are also edible, though most prefer the taste of the bottom white part rather than the upper green part. The inside of a cattail spike contains fluffy seeds that, when dry, make easy fire-starting material (Dayton 2020).

- **Wild asparagus:** Wild asparagus has a thinner stalk than its grocery store counterpart, though this makes it easier to eat raw when necessary. This plant grows wild across North America and Europe and provides a variety of needed nutrients ("Surviving in the Wild" 2020).

- **Dandelion:** Much maligned as a "weed," dandelions provide an excellent nutrition source. All the parts of the dandelion are edible, though young leaves will be less bitter than mature leaves; boil mature leaves and roots before eating. Dandelion flowers are edible, as well ("Surviving in the Wild" 2020).

- **Acorns:** Acorns are ubiquitous in the United States—you can find them wherever oak trees grow. Unlike many natural plant sources, acorns are calorie-dense and contain fat, which can be difficult to access when foraging. To make acorns edible, mash them up and run water through them. You'll know they're ready when their bitter taste has washed away (Dayton 2020).

- **Prickly pear cactus:** One benefit of prickly pear cacti is that they grow in dry areas, where it can be hard to forage or secure adequate hydration. Prickly pear cacti have wide, flat pads and red fruits; the fruit can be eaten raw, while the pads can be peeled and cooked. Be cautious of the durable thorns on both parts of the plant (Chambers 2021).
- **Clover:** Clovers are not necessarily nutritionally exciting —they don't offer much fat, protein, or abundant calories —but they are easy to find and usually grow in large patches. You can eat clover raw, though it is more palatable when cooked (Dayton 2020).

Familiarize yourself with plants that are common in your area to best plan your foraging trips. When harvesting, avoid taking more than a quarter of the plant, as this will reduce regrowth and, thus, the sustainability of the food source. Don't take the "mother" plant, or the largest portion in the middle, or a sole plant, as this will prevent regrowth (Wondersmith 2023).

While you should also acquaint yourself with common dangerous plants in your area—and you should never eat a plant that you can't identify—you should generally avoid any plant that ("Surviving in the Wild" 2020):

- Has milky or discolored sap
- Has thorns, spines, or fine hairs
- Has a bitter or soapy taste
- Has foliage reminiscent of dill, carrot, or parsley
- Has an almond or pear scent
- Has pink, purple, or black spurs
- Has a three-leaf growth pattern

Though plants that possess these characteristics may be fine to eat, many toxic plants exhibit one or more of these attributes. Unless you can identify them as definitely edible (such as dill itself, for example), it's better to steer clear. Don't assume that because an animal eats a plant, you can eat it, too.

If you're in really dire straits and can't find a suitable food source but have access to a plant you think *might* be edible, you can perform the universal edibility test (Demillo Wagner 2021):

1. Separate the plant's roots, stems, leaves, buds, and flowers. Perform this test with only one part of the plant at a time.

2. Smell it. If it smells bad or smells like almond or pear (which can indicate naturally occurring cyanide), discard. If it smells fine, proceed.

3. Test it for contact poisoning. Place a small piece on your inner elbow or wrist for eight hours. If you have any negative effects (burning, itching, numbness, rash, etc.), discard them. If no ill effects occur, proceed.

4. Cook it as you plan to eat it. Boiling is a good test method. Over-boil rather than under-boil, as under-boiling can leave toxins in the plant matter.

5. Touch the plant to your lips to test for burning or itching. If you have no reaction after fifteen minutes, proceed.

6. Take a small bite, chew, and hold it in your mouth for fifteen minutes. If it tastes bitter or soapy (or causes any other negative reactions), spit it out and wash your mouth. If it tastes fine, proceed.

7. Swallow the bite and wait for eight hours. Avoid eating other strange foods during this time. If you have no ill effects, assume this part of the plant (prepared this way) is edible. If you begin to feel sick, induce vomiting to prevent any further symptoms.

Edible Insects

Though eating insects is not widespread in the United States, Canada, or Europe in the present day, using insects as a food source remains a popular option in many other parts of the world, as insects provide an abundant source of protein. Bamboo worms are popular street food in Thailand and Vietnam, while Papua New Guinea eats insects as part of traditional meals (Oliviadese and Dindo 2023).

While U.S. dietary standards may mean that you don't want to make insect eating part of your everyday menu, knowing which of these protein-rich creatures are edible can offer valuable insights during a survival situation.

The following bugs can be foraged and eaten to bolster your diet in an emergency (Louv 2023).

Crickets

These large insects are relatively easy to catch and are widely available, making them a good choice for foragers. You can either catch the insects by hand or by chasing or shaking them onto fabric —wool is best—so that their legs get caught, slowing them down. If you bury a large-mouthed bottle and put overripe fruit or a small light inside (both things that attract crickets), your breakfast will hop right in. Put in a few leaves so the crickets hide instead of trying to escape and leave overnight.

To prepare, pull off the crickets' heads; their entrails should come loose, too. Remove wings and legs, then dry roast in a pan. Cooking reduces risk of parasite transmission.

Ants

Ants are easy to find, and their propensity for straight lines will lead you straight to their anthill (or other home). To forage, hit the anthill with a stick a few times, then poke your stick through the opening. Ants will climb the stick. Dunk the stick into the water to dislodge and drown them. Repeat until you have the desired quantity.

To prepare ants, boil them for about six minutes. To streamline this process, use one heat-resistant container for both dunking and boiling.

Termites

Termites are one of the safest bugs to eat; because they stay buried in wood for nearly all their lifespan, they are less likely to carry parasites than many other insect options. To harvest termites, break open a log and shake them out. Move quickly, as termites will burrow into the wood when light hits them. Roast them in a dry pan to make them edible.

Woodlice

Woodlice (which are known as "potato bugs," "pill bugs," or "rolly pollies" in different regions) are not insects at all—they're crustaceans. Their flavor is often likened to shrimp, making them one of the more delicious forgeable critters. Look for woodlice under rocks or logs.

When you're preparing these land crustaceans, be cautious. Woodlice can carry parasitic roundworms, so they need to be thoroughly boiled before consumption. After cooking, drain out the water and enjoy.

Stinkbugs

While a good rule of thumb is to avoid eating anything that smells bad, stinkbugs are the exception. These bugs, which are widely available across the U.S. year-round, are likely to be found hiding under rocks or logs in winter and parading about during the rest of the year.

To prepare stinkbugs, soak them in water for five to ten minutes to remove the scent that gives these bugs their name. Then, roast in a dry pan.

Hunting and Trapping

Hunting and trapping animal-based foods is a valuable skill, especially in long-term survival situations that extend into winter weather, when plants and bugs may be less abundant or harder to find. Animal-based foods, such as meat, are also nearly universally edible, though they do need to be cooked thoroughly to avoid transmitting bacteria or parasites, and you should never eat an animal that appears sick.

Note that meat takes effort to digest; don't rely on animal food sources if you don't have adequate water. This can lead to hygiene issues when cleaning your kills and will dehydrate you further as your body struggles to find the water needed for digestion (Yost n.d.). Use as many parts of the animal as you can, both out of respect for its lost life and to maximize your own survival benefit.

We'll cover two methods for securing animal food sources: hunting and trapping.

Hunting

When hunting an animal, you will need to both stalk it (though fortune will occasionally put a small animal in your path) and kill it. When stalking an animal, walk slowly and check before you step. The snap of a brittle twig can send your prey bolting. Most animals will eat in between pauses to assess for danger; time your movement to their eating periods when they're less alert (Brown n.d.).

Once you get within range of an animal, you will need to kill it. Experienced hunters may already have a weapon of choice, but if you need to quickly forage a weapon, consider a throwing stick. Look for a stick that is about 2.5 feet long and sturdy enough that it won't break even when thrown or used to strike a small animal. Practice throwing this stick at targets from different angles, aiming to end with your shoulders squared toward your target for maximum impact (Brown n.d.). Aim to make a "clean kill" whenever possible to minimize the animal's suffering (Yost n.d.). Learn the best "kill zones" for the animals you are most likely to hunt in your area.

Trapping

Traps can help you circumvent the need to stalk small animals. Setting traps takes advantage of an animal's movements in the absence of human intervention—and leaves a valuable food source for you to come back to when you're ready. Easy and valuable traps for securing animal-based foods include (MacWelch 2019):

- **Fixed loop snare:** This snare involves looping a solid wire or braided steel cable in a noose-shaped loop. Secure the other end of the wire with a sturdy stick that you can secure into the ground. Place snares over small game trails; when animals pass by, they will become entangled in the snare. The pros of this snare are the ease of building it. Cons include a slower death for the animal and the likelihood that the wire will break or be too disfigured to reuse.

- **Drowning snare:** This snare provides a quick death for animals. To build this snare, tie the snare line to a heavy rock. Set a noose loop in the line. Prop the rock with a stick so that it will fall into a water source if the noose is tugged. Tie a float stick to the far end of the snare line. When an animal is caught in the snare, they will tug, dislodging the rock and sending them into the water. The float stick will indicate where the rock and animal are under the water. This trap will also keep your catch away from scavengers.
- **Rolling snare:** This snare uses "hooks" to trigger the snare. To build, find a forked branch that is about a diameter or two thick. Cut a point on the non-forked side and drive securely into the ground. Find a smaller forked branch and tie it to the snare line. Hook the two forks so that if the snare is jostled, the smaller fork will fall off. Hang the snare with two twigs and place it near a game trail.

GROWING YOUR OWN FOOD

If you've ever found yourself thinking that only people with natural green thumbs can maintain a successful garden, think again. With careful planning and proper guidance, you can grow a prolific garden and provide yourself with one of the best, most enduring ways to sustainably source food.

Crops to Include in Your Garden

First, plan what crops you will want or need. Knowing what you plan to grow, especially if you plan to rely upon your garden as a primary source of sustenance, will help determine other aspects, including the size of your garden plot.

Then, seek crops that are easy to grow, full of sustenance, and offer diverse nutrients. Consider including:

- Potatoes, which require minimal maintenance, thrive in a variety of conditions and can be grown in small spaces. Potatoes, moreover, provide a good source of vitamin C, vitamin B6, potassium, and fiber (Off Grid Dwellings 2023).

- Beans provide dense nutrition in a small, adaptable, and easy-to-preserve package. Many beans can also grow vertically, which can save space in narrow garden beds. Edible pod beans can provide double the nutrition with virtually no wasted plant material (Nielsen 2020).

- Squash is great for planning year-round food sources from your garden. Summer squash grows quickly, while winter squash, though slower to grow, can be stored whole for extended periods of time. Squash also grows well when interspersed with beans and corn, thus maximizing the square footage of your garden (Nielsen 2020).

- Cabbage can be planted in spring or fall, as this hearty vegetable thrives in cool weather. Cabbage is versatile, nutritious, and long-lasting, especially when preserved. Fermented cabbage will make sauerkraut, which promotes gut health, and pickled cabbage, such as kimchi, adds a flavorful kick to meals (Off Grid Dwellings 2023).

- Berries provide a much-needed source of sugar and sweetness, which can be hard to come by when cultivating or foraging for food. Space restrictions may affect your choice. Strawberries, for example, like to spread, while raspberries and blueberries spring up on bushes, making them more compact (Nielsen 2020).

- Herbs grow in small spaces and add flavor to your dishes. Think this isn't important? Try eating bland, unseasoned foods for a meal or two, then check to see how that affects your mood and overall well-being.

Other good survival garden choices include carrots, beets, radishes, tomatoes, sweet potatoes, onions, garlic, collard greens, cucumbers, spinach, Swiss chard, broccoli, and lettuce (Jackson 2023).

Planning Your Survival Garden

When planning your garden, first consider your family's needs. As a general rule, consider that you need about 150 square feet for a family of two, then an additional hundred square feet for each additional family member. Thus, a family of four would need about 350 square feet, while a family of six would need about 550 square feet (Jackson 2023).

From there, consider how much of your food you intend to get from your garden so that you can determine how many calories need to come from crops you grow. Estimate that each member of your family needs about 2,000 calories each day, then calculate how much of each crop you wish to cultivate based on those needs. It takes a quarter of a pound of dried beans, on average, to produce five hundred calories, while equivalent calories come from just over one pound of potatoes and about two pounds of winter squash (Team New Terra n.d.). If you prefer lower-calorie vegetables or those with more limited yields per square foot, you might need a larger garden than what is estimated above.

Once you've determined the size you need, determine a good location for your garden. This location should consider sun exposure; if you're planting near your house, choose land that faces south to maximize sunlight (Spahr and Spahr 2023). Seek a flat area that can be enclosed if local wildlife finds your garden and decides it looks like a good source of tasty snacks. Make sure you have adequate access to water to keep your plants with the hydration they need.

Raised Bed Gardening Basics

Raised bed gardening helps you maximize your rich gardening soil by keeping it contained. Raised beds also add convenience, especially for those who have back issues—their increased height makes them easier to access and inspect for pests.

Raised beds do have some downsides. They can be expensive to build, though using recycled wood can help you minimize costs. Raised soil is also more susceptible to heat and cold fluctuations, especially if the walls of your bed are thin. This, on its own, can be good and bad: while your plants will be more susceptible to frost, they will also warm earlier and give you a longer growing season (Gardener's Supply 2024). You will also lose some real estate due to the required space between beds (Lamp'l 2018).

To winterize gardening beds, remove all "spent" vegetables, as these can lead to sprouting weeds in spring. Wrap perennials to protect them from frost. You can also plant "cover crops" about a month before your first estimated frost date in order to benefit from your beds during the winter and help prevent weeds come spring (Nolan 2021).

Building Raised Beds

To build raised beds (Nemett 2021):

1. Prepare your build site by digging out the top layer of grass, any rocks or roots, and by leveling the ground so your bed will sit on flat land.

2. Cut boards to the size of the bed you intend to build.

3. Build the boards into a rectangle. Check again to ensure they are level, as boards that are askew will compound problems as you build.

4. Fasten corners of the lowest level rectangle, then add in corner stakes to add your second row of boards atop the first.

5. Add in more stakes along the sides of the bed. Add a third level

of boards if you desire additional height, then trip the stakes so they don't extend higher than the sides of the bed.

6. (Optional) Add a lip, securing to corners and each stake.

7. Repeat for as many beds as your garden requires.

Fill each bed with six to eighteen inches of soil according to the pH, texture, and drainage needs of the plants you desire to grow.

Companion Planting

Companion planting is a system that involves combing compatible plants to increase soil nutrients, discourage pets, and maximize the space in your garden. The following table will illustrate what are good companion plants for crops that you may desire in your survival garden, as well as plants which do not do well as neighbors (Malinoski 2018).

Plant Name	Companion Plants	Plants to Avoid in the Same Space
Brassicas family plants (broccoli, Brussels sprouts, cabbage)	Celery, beans, beets, dill, lettuce	Tomatoes, eggplant, peppers, squash
Carrot	Tomatoes, leeks, rosemary, sage, chives	Coriander, dill, parsnips
Potatoes	Beans, cabbage, eggplant, peas, corn, marigolds, horseradish	Tomatoes
Summer squash	Beans, peas, radishes, peppermint, dill, parsley, oregano	Potatoes, cucumbers
Sweet corn	Beans, cucumbers, peas, melons, zucchini	Tomatoes
Tomato	Basil, marigolds, asparagus, celery, lettuce, spinach, onions	Cabbage, beets, peas, rosemary, potatoes
Winter squash	Corn, beans, sunflowers	Radishes (or other root crops)

Companion Planting Chart

Crop Rotation

Crop rotation reduces damage from insects, manages soil fertility, and limits vegetable diseases by changing the planting location of different vegetables for each season. Rotating crops depends on not putting crops in the same "families" in the same location year after year. Plant families are organized as follows (Higgins and Krokowski 2012):

Plant Family	Vegetables
Carrot family	Carrot, celery, parsnip, parsley
Goosefoot family	Beet, spinach, Swiss chard
Gourd family	Cucumber, pumpkin, summer squash, watermelon, winter squash
Mustard family	Broccoli, Brussels sprouts, cabbage, cauliflower, collard greens, kale, kohlrabi, mustard greens, radish, rutabaga, turnip
Nightshade family	Eggplant, pepper, potato, tomato
Onion family	Chives, garlic, leek, onion
Pea family	Bush bean, kidney bean, lima bean, pea, soybean
Sunflower family	Endive, lettuce, sunflower

Crop Rotation Chart

Accounting for crop rotation within families can require planning in advance, especially for gardens with little extra space. Tomatoes and potatoes, for example, do not plant well together, but you also cannot swap them in a single container in successive seasons, as they're part of the same plant family.

Garden Troubleshooting

Even the most accomplished gardeners kill plants sometimes. That said, when you're gardening for food, you want to maximize your yield each growing season. Consider the following common problems in your garden, as well as strategies for how to fix them (Judd 2022).

If your plants are weak and growing poorly, this might be due to weeds "choking" out light or nutrients. Try pulling weeds. This same poor growth can be caused by poor soil, which can be improved with compost or fertilization, or lack of sunlight, which can be fixed by moving beds.

If plants look dry and their edges are curling, wind is likely the source. Add windbreaks to protect plants. Burned or yellow leaves indicate excess sun; provide shade, particularly in hot months. If leaves are brown and dry, especially lower leaves, the plants are underwatered. If your plants look wilted and have new growth falling off, by contrast, you may be overwatering soil and need to let it dry between watering. Consider a moisture meter to help judge soil moisture levels.

While foraging, gardening, and hunting can meet a great deal of your sustenance needs, these food sources may become scarcer in winter months, particularly if there is no small game near your home. In the next chapter, we'll discuss how keeping livestock—and learning the basics of animal husbandry—can keep you safe from seasonal fluctuations in plant availability.

5

CHAPTER FIVE—L: LEVERAGE YOUR LIVESTOCK AND FOOD STOCK

Raising livestock is a valuable way to maintain a consistent food supply year-round. Depending on which animals you raise, you can get eggs, milk...and meat. Securing meat from livestock requires butchering animals; however, this is something that many animal husbandry novices find unsettling to contemplate.

Feeling queasy about butchering animals does not mean that you are destined to fail in an off-grid setting, nor does it mean that you are weak or undisciplined. Those who are familiar with the unfortunate necessity of butchering animals for food often commiserate over their initial struggles with killing animals and advise familiarizing themselves with different methods for humane slaughter. Other advice is to read books like Temple Grandin's Animals Make Us Human, which can help you embrace how you can have compassion for animals even when you rely upon them for food.

In this chapter, we'll explore practical tips for animal husbandry, how to best raise and feed animals, and how you can build these habits into a self-sustaining farm that maximizes the utility of the animals whose lives are sacrificed for your survival.

ANIMAL HUSBANDRY

Animal husbandry, or practices of raising domestic animals for food, protection, or land management, is thousands of years old. While many animals can be helpful when living off the grid, there are varying degrees of difficulty and benefits when it comes to raising animals for food.

When it comes to raising livestock, consider your space constraints. One acre of land, for example, can support a dairy cow, two goats, several pigs, and about a dozen hens (Seymour 2023). This can provide milk, meat, eggs, and manure that will help grow your crops. You can also think about your space on a per-animal basis, a method often beneficial for smaller homesteads. Chickens, for example, need about ten square feet per bird outside and three square feet per bird inside the coop. If you plan to grow the grain to feed your animals, however, that should be included in your space calculations. To grow sufficient grain for a single hen, for example, you will need about 1,000 square feet of growth (Waddington 2024).

Chickens

Raising chickens is a common first stop when raising animals for food, and for a good reason—chickens can, when happy and protected from predators, lay hundreds of eggs per year per laying hen (Magyar 2023). Chickens are also foragers who will eat bugs out of your garden, and chicken feces can be composted. Cons to keeping chickens? They're noisy, especially early in the morning, so they may disturb you early in the morning. Chickens are also prone to disease more than some other animals (Magyar 2023).

Ducks

Ducks are less common than chickens, though many farmers who have kept both claim that they prefer to raise ducks, which can be less noisy (Coosemans 2021). Ducks have many of the same benefits as chickens—they will eat pests and are happy in small areas—though ducks will also require a small pond. Ducks layer fewer eggs than chickens, but these eggs are more nutritionally dense (Magyar 2023).

Rabbits

Rabbits are one of the fastest reproducers in the animal kingdom, which helps their status as a sustainable food source animal. Mature rabbits can produce several litters per year as they only gestate for about a month. They're also cost-effective and quiet, provide useful manure, and can live in small spaces. Their fur and skins can also be used or cut, in the case of Angora rabbits (Magyar 2023). Rabbits need protection from predators, and their cages need frequent cleaning. Their meat may also be an acquired taste.

Goats

The distinctive, noisy bleating of goats may be easy to disregard when you learn that goats provide meat, fiber, and milk—and can be kept in a smaller area than cows, another milk producer. Goats can also help manage your land, as they'll eat weeds and brush—though they can also prove picky eaters. Goats are clever and will escape their enclosure, and therefore, overall, require more care than poultry or small animals (Magyar 2023).

Tips on Raising Healthy Livestock

Maintaining livestock requires a great deal of preparation, as each species of animal will have its own needs regarding feeding, housing, and terrain. To start, ensure that you have secure and safe housing for your animals. Give animals enough space to move around freely and ensure that they have adequate access to water and shelter. Smaller animals like chickens and rabbits will require more secure coops or hutches, as they are in danger of predation (Survival Jack 2023). Secure fencing will also keep your animals safe from larger predators and on your land instead of having them wander away.

Consider your climate; certain chicken breeds, for example, do not do well in cold weather, which may make them a poor choice depending on where you live (Survival Jack 2023). Plan for waste disposal so that feces do not risk your family's or your livestock's water supply, which can lead to disease. Consult a veterinarian, keeping in mind that a local vet who specializes in cats and dogs may not have the correct training to treat livestock, especially larger animals like pigs, horses, or cows.

Building a Chicken Coop

In addition to chickens being one of the easier animals to raise, chicken coops are one of the easiest animal enclosures to build. Chickens need a structure that will keep them safe from predators, dry in inclement weather, warm in winter, and cool in summer—but beyond that, you can make a coop however you like, including from recycled or reclaimed materials. Consider how long you want your coop to last when choosing these materials, as solid timber will last longer than bird or mouse wire.

To build a chicken coop (Dine-a-Chook 2023):

1. Frame three sides of the chicken coop by taking timber pallets or used doors and screwing them together. If you plan to add a floor, do it at this point. If your land is sufficiently dry, even during rain, you may choose to use sand as a base layer for your coop instead of building a floor.

2. (Optional) Add a window, such as from a glass door or unframed windows, to allow chickens more light and to give you greater visibility.

3. Add a door. If you plan to access the coop infrequently, consider adding a chicken-sized door as well as one big enough for human entry. Using the smaller door when only chickens need to access the coop will keep the insides secure and comfortable for the chickens.

4. Use tall poles or other timber to build the four corners taller. Build up siding using wood, sheet metal, or melamine. Add wire to any gaps and seal with builder's foam. If you live in a cold climate, seek materials with greater insulation; if you live in a hot area, add more ventilation holes, which should be covered with wire (note that the holes in chicken wire are too big to protect from many snakes).

5. Add in nesting materials. Recycled pet carriers, old drawers, baskets, milk crates, or plastic tubs can be used as nesting boxes, while you can use ladders or fence pickets screwed to the sides of the coop to create roosts.

6. Add a roof made of timber, old roofing, or sheet metal or plastic. Screw tightly to frames and sides of the coop, sealing gaps with wire and builder's foam.

PROCESSING MEAT

Processing meat is frequently the part of livestock raising that even seasoned homesteaders find unpleasant. Knowing how to humanely butcher different types of animals, however, can streamline this process, making it faster and more sanitary.

Chickens

Homesteaders debate the best process for butchering a chicken; the FDA offers no official recommendation for humane chicken slaughter (U.S. Department of Agriculture n.d.). Slicing the carotid artery is one quick and minimally painful way to kill chickens. To cull chickens according to this method (Lobermeier 2022):

1. Restrict the chickens' food intake for twelve to twenty-four hours before beginning the butchering process. This will keep their intestines empty during the butchering process.

2. Attach a culling cone to a sturdy tree or fence post. These cones look like inverted triangles prevent poultry from flapping violently and hurting themselves during butchering. Attach the cone so the narrow end is pointed down and you can access both the top and the bottom of the cone easily. Place a bucket beneath the cone to catch blood.

3. Stun the chicken by grabbing its body and pressing its wings to the side. Use a swirling motion to move the chicken in front of you. This will disorient the chicken, making it easier to insert them in the cone. Once disoriented, put the chicken headfirst into the cone.

4. Using a sharp knife, make a horizontal cut across the chicken's

entire neck, just below the jawbone. You should see two streams of blood emerging in an inverted V shape; this means that both carotid arteries were severed. If the blood flow is slow, you have not cut deep enough. Let the bird bleed for at least three minutes, then confirm it is dead. If you are uncertain, you can decapitate the chicken to confirm death.

5. Clean the chicken carcass and culling cone with diluted bleach; chickens frequently defecate during death.

6. De-feather the chicken by dunking it into a stock pot filled with water at a rolling boil. Hold the chicken by its feet and dunk to where the feathers end. Dunk for one to two seconds, pull it out of the water, then repeat the dunking. Let the water drip from the carcass.

7. On a sanitized workspace, use your fingers to pull feathers loose by pulling in the opposite direction from growth.

8. To eviscerate the chicken, first remove the feet by cutting through the foot joint. Set aside; chicken feet are edible.

9. Next, make a cut in the throat skin to reveal the neck muscles. Pull the skin over the top of the neck so it falls to the back of the chicken. The ribbed windpipe, or trachea, and the esophagus are located and are connected to a sack under the skin on the right breast. This sack is the crop, which should be empty, as it is part of the digestive tract. If the crop is full, be careful not to break it, as the contents can contaminate your meat. If the crop breaks, spray away its contents immediately. Detach the crop from the breast meat by severing the thin connective membrane. Cut away the trachea and esophagus as far into the chicken's chest as you can. Discard these scraps.

10. Make a small cut through the vertebrae above the tail and oil gland, slicing until the vertebrae separate. Use caution to avoid cutting through the intestines. When you see the intestines, cut along the side of the tail and rectum, inside the pelvic bone, then flip the chicken so the breast is facing up. Cut under the bones of the ribcage with kitchen scissors until you can see the internal organs.

Slice along the side of the ribcage to meet the cuts you made on the tail side. Reach inside the chicken and remove the organs, which should still be attached to one another. If you cut the intestines, you will be able to tell due to the smell of feces. If this occurs, wash your chicken immediately.

11. Once you remove the organs, you can either leave the chicken whole or cut it into smaller parts before putting it in an ice bath to prohibit bacterial growth.

Rabbit

As with chickens, there are several ways to slaughter rabbits quickly. We'll discuss the stick method, which involves stunning the rabbit before breaking its neck. To butcher a rabbit using this method (Traister 2024):

1. Stun the rabbit by striking it hard in the back of its neck behind the ears. Place the rabbit on the ground, place the stick horizontally over its neck, and step on either side of the stick to hold it in place. Then, hold the rabbit by its hind legs and pull up sharply to disconnect the cervical vertebrae. Doing so quickly kills the rabbit before it wakes up from being stunned, which avoids pain or trauma to the animal.

2. Hang the rabbit by its hind legs so that its head dangles down. The disconnected vertebrae will leave a gap between the neck bones; you can use a knife in this gap to sever the head.

3. Carefully cut through the skin along the hind leg joints. Rabbit skin is thin; avoid cutting muscles or tendons. Once you've done this on both hind legs, cut the skin inside the legs in a V shape toward the anus and around it. Then, peel the skin down the body of the rabbit. This fur can be kept and tanned. Clip off the front feet with shears.

4. Next, remove the bladder by cutting the abdomen open. Avoid cutting the intestines. Pull out the bladder below the meat so your meat won't be compromised by urine if the bladder ops.

5. Break the bone between the two hind legs, cut around the anus, and remove it and the intestines together.

6. Remove the back feet with shears and wash the remaining

meat in cold water. Put the meat in a plastic bag and let it chill for twenty-four hours in a cooler filled with ice.

Pig

According to the Humane Methods of Slaughter Act, larger live-stock, including cows and pigs, must be killed using rapid and effective methods that make them "insensible to pain," except for when killed according to religious practices (National Agricultural Library n.d.). Experts from the South Dakota State University recommend using a .22 caliber rifle for humane swine slaughter, though they caution that this should only be done if you can use the weapon safely.

To butcher a pig according to these protocols (Blair and Baker 2023):

1. Separate the pig you intend to slaughter from other livestock. Consider choosing to work on an incline so blood flows away from your workspace. Choose an area small enough that the pig cannot run and that you can get a clear, accurate shot.

2. Stun the pig by shooting it in the center of the forehead, approximately an inch and a half above the eyes. Ideally, you should penetrate the brain on the first shot but ensure that you have a backup round ready to complete the stunning. When properly stunned, the pig will not make a sound, will not breathe rhythmically, and will not blink if you touch their eye. Rapid leg movement does not signify a failed stun; this is caused by nervous system disruption due to the stun.

3. Roll the pig over to access its underside. Locate the sternum where the front ribs meet the legs, then trace toward the head to find the end of the sternum. Insert your knife behind the sternum, pointing the knife tip toward the tail and the sharp edge toward the backbone so that the knife is behind and parallel to the sternum. Flick your wrist to turn the blade forty-five degrees, then withdraw the knife. Blood should flow out quickly, indicating a severed carotid artery. If you don't see rapid blood flow, repeat the motion with the knife.

4. Use a thick rope or chain around the hocks, looping behind the dewclaws, being careful to ensure that the ropes don't slip as you raise the carcass completely off the ground. A tractor can help you maneuver the pig's weight. Rise the carcass and scrub with a bristle brush.

5. Scald the carcass in water heated to 145-150 degrees. Don't let the carcass sit on the bottom of the container, or the meat and skin will begin to cook. Move the pig continuously. After a few minutes, the hair will begin to peel easily. Remove the carcass from the water and scrape against the direction of hair growth to remove as much hair as possible. If you do not have a container large enough to allow a dip scald, you can replicate this effect by pouring hot water over old towels that cover the carcass. When the hair is fully removed, rinse and brush the carcass again.

6. Remove the head by facing the carcass' back and making a cut above the skull to expose the vertebrae. Insert your knife between the skull and the vertebrae to sever the M-shaped joint. Cut above the Adam's apple to facilitate removing the internal organs. For a male pig, remove the penis by cutting through the skin where the back legs meet. Cut toward the navel, taking an off-center path to avoid severing the penis and contaminating it with urine. You will be able to see a long white structure about an inch in diameter; once you get close to the navel, pull this structure toward you and cut behind it to separate it from the body wall. Repeat this as you move toward the anus; when you reach the back point, you can remove the penis from the carcass.

7. To eviscerate the pig, cut around the anus, giving an inch of clearance to avoid puncturing the rectum. Cut the tissues that hold the rectum in place. On the belly side, score the skin from the back legs to the sternum, then repeat the gesture to open the body cavity. Avoid stabbing, which can puncture organs. Insert your hand, knife blade facing out, then cut down the length of the body. Doing so with your hand and the knife blade on the inside will prevent you from puncturing your intestines.

8. Use a zip tie to close the anus to prevent fecal contamination. Then, pull the organs forward and out of the body. Use your knife to cut through any heavy connective tissue. Use your hand to follow the esophagus; once this is cut free from the trachea, the digestive organs should be easily removed. Cut the large vein that runs along the backbone, then hold the vein to cut toward the head, along the backbone. Remove the heart, lungs, and trachea. Inspect the organs for any signs of illness or infection.

9. Remove the large amount of "leaf fat" that lines the abdominal cavity. This can be used to make lard.

10. Split the carcass using your knife or a saw. Inspect the carcass for signs of contamination. Rise off the carcass using hot water. Let it drip, then spray it with a white vinegar and water solution that uses two parts vinegar for every three parts of water. Cool the carcass.

MAKING YOUR FOOD LAST

Preserving food is an essential element in off-grid living, as plant-based foods will be available fresh on seasonal cycles, and meat can spoil quickly if not properly treated and stored. Consider the following methods, many of which use little or no electricity, to preserve your food and make stores last longer.

Canning

Canning is one of the most versatile preservation methods, as it can be used for both low- and high-acid foods. When you can food, you seal it in cans or jars, then heat these containers using boiling water (high-acid foods) or pressure heating (low-acid foods), which kills any remaining bacteria (Nicolaides 2021). Pros of canning include the ability to eat food immediately after it has been canned and the reusability of most canning equipment. Cons include expensive start-up costs and the potential to create a breeding ground for botulism if the canning process is done incorrectly. If a can buckles outward or shows signs of yeasts or molds, dispose of it; do not eat the contents. If you eat canned food and have trouble swallowing, muscle weakness, blurry vision, or slurred speech, go to the emergency room immediately (CDC 2021).

Pickling

Pickling is a millennia-old technique for food preservation that involves immersing food in edible acids or fermenting them. The high acid used in pickling (vinegar is the most common option) prohibits bacteria growth by elevating the natural acidity of the food you are preserving (Nicolaides 2021). The pros of pickling are its versatility; you can pickle meat, vegetables, and fruits to preserve them. Pickling also requires less special equipment than canning. Cons include the longer time investment, as pickling, depending on what you are seeking to preserve, needs to be done days or weeks before you are preparing to eat the food. Note that some foods that can be pickled, such as hard-boiled eggs, still need to be kept refrigerated to keep them safe to consume (Sakawsky 2017).

Dehydrating

Dehydrating foods has dual benefits: removing moisture makes it much harder for mold or bacteria to grow, and the dried food is highly portable (Nicolaides 2021). You can dehydrate foods in commercially available food dehydrators or by cooking them for a long time on low heat in your oven. You can also make a solar-operated food dehydrator by building a structure with a dark metal bottom and a glass top that opens. Keep the structure shallow to allow heat from the sun to maximally heat the space. These dehydrators work best in environments with low humidity and on foods that breed bacteria more slowly (fruit or vegetables instead of meat [Palethorphe 2019]).

Curing

To cure meats, you use salt to remove the moisture that allows for bacteria growth. You can cure using two methods: dry curing, which involves covering the meat with salt for an entire day, or equilibrium curing, a method that uses less salt. To equilibrium cure, weigh the meat, then cover it with an amount of salt that weighs three percent of the meat's weight. Use a vacuum sealer to remove air and let sit in the refrigerator for approximately five days (Web-staurantStore 2024).

Smoking

Smoking meat involves cooking it in a smoky space in low heat for hours or days. To smoke meat, remove excess fat that won't be absorbed into the meat. Then, truss any loose flaps to prevent them from cooking too quickly. Suspend this above-smoking wood of your choice for as long as it takes to cook. You can also smoke some cheese and vegetables (Keith 2020).

Pros of smoking involve the complex flavors you can achieve and the low cost of getting started. Cons include the long cooking times.

Some of the survival techniques we've discussed thus far in this book are low- or no-energy, while others require some electricity to set up. In the next chapter, we'll discuss how to adopt practical energy solutions so that you can maximize your quality of life without relying on the electric company.

TOGETHER, WE ARE STRONGER

"I envision a day when every city and town has front and backyards... nurtured into life by neighbors who are no longer strangers, but friends who delight in the edible rewards offered from a garden they discovered together."

— *GREG PETERSON*

No-grid survival is often pictured as a lonely pursuit; one in which each person is for themselves and competition rather than companionship prevails. But it doesn't have to be that way and in fact, in emergency situations in which the power suddenly goes out, the greatest strength you find lies in unity. In Chapter 4, we focused on foraging for food and growing thriving fruit and vegetable gardens. Can you imagine forming part of a community in which everyone specializes in something... be it foraging for mushrooms, growing citrus fruits, or harvesting root vegetables?

We are all potential experts. Each of us has talents, abilities, and skills, often passed on from previous generations. In a disaster situation, our chances of survival rise when we share our knowledge and take on specialized tasks that allow our families or small communities to thrive in diversity. Imagine a situation in which you and your neighbors grow and trade specific produce, sharing everything from freshly picked tomatoes and peppers to pickled delights that last through various seasons. This is exactly what I envisioned when I decided to write this book; a situation in which entire communities work together so everyone knows what to do if they are "thrust into darkness." When each of us carries a torch, we can illuminate a village, town, or street. And you can start building this community right now, by simply letting others know what you think of this book.

By leaving a review of this book on Amazon, you can help new readers harness a vital list of preparedness skills that will help them form part of a caring, supportive community.

Thanks for not just believing in the power of information but also sharing it.

6

CHAPTER SIX—A: AMP UP YOUR ENERGY INDEPENDENCE

Renewable energy often feels like a modern, or even futuristic, concept. But the concept of renewable energy was actually introduced in 1873 by Augustin Mouchot, who invented the solar-powered engine. Renewable energy isn't as impossible to implement as it may seem, either; one wind turbine can power 1,400 homes, and the WWF estimates that the whole planet could be powered by renewable energy by 2050 (myenergi 2022).

In this chapter, we'll discuss how to harness, store, and maintain reliable sources of energy so that you can meet your family's needs, even when living entirely off the grid.

WHY RENEWABLE ENERGY?

What makes renewable energy, or energy from natural and sustainable sources such as the sun or wind, such a good option for off-grid living? Well, most renewable energy sources are widely available, which makes them easier to access than fossil fuels or other forms of energy that cannot be processed at home. Renewable energy sources also integrate easily into daily life, save money over time, and are typically low-maintenance (Veterans Off-Grid 2020). Incorporating these systems is often the best way to establish energy independence, sparing you from being reliant on larger systems to provide your energy needs.

PLANNING YOUR RENEWABLE ENERGY SYSTEM

To determine your what renewable energy system will work best for your family, you must first determine your energy needs. This should consider fluctuations in your energy needs throughout the day and over the course of a year; if you live in a cold climate, for example, you will need more electricity to provide heat in the winter months than you do in the summer. To measure your energy load, calculate how many appliances regularly run in your home, then multiply the wattage of each appliance by the number of hours it is used daily (Energy Saver n.d.). This power data is generally found on a sticker or plate attached to the appliance. Consider what energy-reducing measures you can reasonably implement in your home.

Check local ordinances about what you can or cannot do to your property. Aesthetic or noise-regulation ordinances may limit what renewable energy systems you can implement. Consider seeking an easement that will protect your right to use your land in a way that allows for renewable energy acquisition.

Next, consider what renewable energy resources are available, what size system you will need given your energy consumption, and the cost and other installation considerations before choosing what energy system works for you. We'll discuss common options, how to install different systems, and the pros and cons of each.

Solar Energy

Solar energy is most commonly collected through solar panels (frequently placed on your roof), which convert sunlight into electricity for immediate use or storage. Solar panels convert the sun's photovoltaic effect into direct current (DC) and alternate current (AC) electricity (Solar Learning Center n.d.).

Solar energy can be used to power nearly everything in your home, including providing electricity, heating water and air, circulating water, and cooking (Gordon 2023). Before deciding on solar energy, assess your solar potential. Tools like the National Solar Radiation Database can provide readings on potential solar power in your area. You should also consider more micro factors like shade trees or the age of your roof (Energy Saver n.d.). Using your energy load assessment, determine the number of solar panels you will need to fully cover or defray energy needs to the level you desire.

Next, determine if you prefer roof-mounted or ground solar panels. Roof panels will require more emergency equipment to protect your home in the case of malfunction, while ground panels will occupy more space. Roof panels are generally more expensive to implement and more challenging to maintain, especially if you live in an area where you see abundant snowfall (which needs to be removed from solar panels as quickly as possible to maximize their energy potential. Ground panels are generally easier to install by yourself, which will reduce installation costs (Mack 2024).

To build your own solar energy system (PROINSO n.d.):

1. Select your battery and solar panels. A deep cycle battery will store energy and ensure that your home has power even when the sun isn't shining. For a smaller house, you may be able to use a 12 V or 24 V system, while a larger home may require a 48 V system. Next, select adequate solar panels to fully charge your selected battery in one day.

2.Select a charge controller. While simple on/off controllers work, they are generally less useful at regulating the current and voltage coming from the solar panel than a PWM controller, which is more affordable, or an MPPT controller, which is the most efficient but expensive option.

3.Select an inverter that converts DC into AC. Your inverter's power should be equal to or higher than your energy load. Pure sine wave inverters are most effective, as they work for most appliances, unlike square wave or modified sine wave inverters.

4.Securely mount the solar panel so that they are facing south (if you're in the northern hemisphere) or north (if you're in the southern hemisphere) to maximize sun exposure. Follow the panels' instructions for mounting or use poured concrete to attach the legs of the stand to the ground.

5.Connect the charge controller to the battery using the wires from the solar panels' junction box using an MC4 connector. Ensure that the panel is covered for this connection to avoid damaging the controller with a sudden high voltage.

6.Connect the solar panels to your battery using series connection (to connect the positive terminal of once device to the negative of another) and parallel connection (to connect the positive terminal of once device to the positive of the other).

Wind Energy

Wind turbines can provide renewable energy on a mass scale in windy areas. While full-scale wind turbines provide the most energy, their large size (typically around 100 feet tall) means that they are not legal or practical in many residential areas. Smaller wind turbines, such as roof-mounted turbines or micro domestic turbines, may be more suitable if you don't have a large area of land for a full-scale turbine. While you are likely more familiar with horizontal-axis turbines, which have large blades, you can also save space with a vertical-axis turbine, which has blades that mimic the shape of a whisk blender (Deziel 2024).

Pros to wind energy include their efficiency; wind turbines convert to electricity at a fifty percent rate, while the average solar panel converts at around twenty percent (Deziel 2024). They also can generate energy at night, so long as the wind is blowing. Cons to wind turbines include their visual impact, high installation costs, and need for regular maintenance.

Wind turbines are best suited for rural properties that have high energy needs and are located in windy areas. The National Oceanic and Atmospheric Administration keeps wind maps that show long- and short-term wind rates in different areas; this can help you determine if your area gets enough wind to make wind energy practical. Note that wind turbines work best on a large scale; small wind turbines are cheaper to install, but they are unlikely to provide significant energy (Vaccaro 2024). Wind turbines cost approximately $3,000-$5,000 per kilowatt of capacity, meaning that an average household should expect $15,000-$75,000 in start-up costs, though installation and permits may make this cost higher (Vaccaro 2024).

Biomass Systems

Biomass systems generate energy from burning organic matter, including manure and household waste, though wood fuel is the most common option. When considering a biomass heating system, you will need to choose between a boiler, which can heat radiators for a whole house, or stoves, which heat single rooms. Note that wood boilers are physically larger than oil or gas counterparts and require a flue to let smoke escape your home (Energy Saving Trust n.d.). Biomass systems are currently more popular in the U.K. than in the U.S., where installation costs range from $7,500-$16,000, depending on your location. You will also need to account for fuel costs (Bartolone 2022).

Biogas Systems

Biogas is produced when bacteria break down organic materials (like animal waste and food scraps) in the absence of oxygen. Biogas reduces waste and generates organic fertilizer as a byproduct, which can then be used to foster growth in your garden. Because biogas relies on a biological process, it is not entirely predictable, however, and it works best in warm climates ("What is Biogas?" 2024).

Animal manure, plant material, and food waste can all be used to make biogas, but due to the high risk of contamination, human waste should be recycled using a composting toilet instead (National Grid Group 2023). To make biogas at home ("How to Make Biogas" 2024):

1. Create a biogas digester. This should be a sealed container that can be made from concrete, metal, or plastic. The material must

withstand internal pressure and keep oxygen out. Seek a container with at least 185 gallons of capacity.

2. Connect an inlet system that lets you put organic waste into the dispenser. PVC pipe with a three-inch diameter works well. Attach and seal this to the side of your container near the top. Create a cap to close the inlet system.

3. Connect a stirring system (either manual or mechanical) to prevent the formation of floating layers and accelerate fermentation.

4. Connect a gas collection system that consists of a gas outlet pipe that leads to your gas collection system via a gas valve. This should be attached and sealed to the top of your digester. The containment system can be any airtight container, including one made from flexible materials.

5. Attach a digestate outlet system (a PVC pipe works here, too) to the side of your container near the bottom. This helps extract digestate for use as fertilizer.

6. Load and mix waste and water into the digester to make a slurry. Experiment with water to waste ratios, using 70-80% moisture ratio as a basis, as this leads to maximum efficiency of biogas production.

7. Let the biogas accumulate over days or weeks. Keep the temperature between 85-100 degrees Fahrenheit and the pH level between 6.5 and 8.0. Ensure that gas valves are closed before removing your gas collection system to avoid losing your biogas. You can then attach your collected gas to gas burners, stoves, or generators.

Micro Hydroelectric Systems

If you have a river or spring near your home, you can use this to generate electricity using a water wheel, pump, or turbine. As with wind turbines, micro-hydroelectric systems take the force of the running water and convert it into renewable energy. The most common way to channel water into energy for home use is via a pump or turbine. Pumps are most widely available and are generally more affordable, though they require more maintenance than turbines. Turbines are more efficient, but they are also more expensive and may not work in slow-flow water (Off-Grid Collective n.d.).

Pros of hydroelectric systems include their low operating costs, minimal environmental impacts, and sustainability. Cons include their location limitations, as they must be near suitable water sources and upfront costs. Estimating your water's energy potential is a two-person job. To estimate if your water source is suitable for energy production (Off-Grid Collective n.d.):

1. Stretch a small-diameter flexible tube (such as a garden hose) along your water source. The top of the tube should be at the highest practical elevation point, while the bottom of the tube should reach at least ten feet downstream. Insert a funnel into the top of the tube and hold it underwater as close to the surface as possible.

2. Lift the downstream end of the tube until water no longer flows out. Measure the distance between the tube and the surface of the water. This is the **gross head** for this part of the stream. Mark your location.

3. Repeat steps 1-2, starting with the upstream end of the tube where you marked your place with the downstream end in the previous step. Continue these measurements until you reach the place where you plan to situate your turbine. The average of the measurements gives you the **average gross head** for your hydropower system.

4. Seek part of the stream with a straight channel and uniform width and depth. Measure the width at the narrowest point. Then, measure the depth at various intervals, marking your measurements on graph paper. Use these measurements to calculate the areas of the sections.

5. Find a place at least six meters upstream from where you measured the width. Drop a weighted float (such as a half-full plastic water bottle) in the middle of the stream, then use a stopwatch to determine how long it takes to float to the origin point. Repeat several times for precise measurements. Divide the distance

by the seconds it takes to travel to get the **average velocity** of the water. Multiply this by the area you measured.

6. Multiply for roughness (0.8 for sandy streambeds, 0.7 for small stones, 0.6 for large stones) to get the **flow rate** in cubic meters per second.

7. Multiply the **gross head** x **flow rate**, then divide by ten. This will give you the approximate system output in watts.

ENERGY MANAGEMENT AND BATTERY STORAGE

Off-grid energy sources are often dependent on natural resources, which wax and wane with changes in weather and the seasons. Relying on such systems means that, unless you are willing to only have power when it's sunny, windy, or when your creek is flowing with force, you will need to be able to store excess energy in times of plenty so you can continue to access electricity and heat consistently. This means investing in a home battery system.

Home batteries are different from the small cell batteries that go in kids' toys. Recent developments in lithium-ion battery technology have made batteries highly efficient, scalable, and lightweight. There are two main types of home battery systems (Svarc n.d.):

- **All-in-one battery energy storage systems (BESS)** are the most cost-effective option. They contain an inverter, charger, and connection (most commonly to a solar power system) in a single unit.
- **Modular DC battery systems** connect to a separate DC battery system and function as a highly flexible hybrid inverter for your home energy. They come in a wider range of sizes, which makes them suitable for more households.

Home battery systems keep you in power even when you face a blackout or emergency and can reduce electric bills, as they can effectively store excess solar, hydro, or wind energy. Implementing a home battery system does generally have a high installation cost, however.

When choosing a home battery system, you need to consider numerous factors (Harden 2024):

1. How much energy does your home use in an average day? This will help you understand what capacity your battery needs. This is measured in kilowatt-hours or kWh.

2. How much energy do you use at once? This will affect your needed power output, which will be higher if you plan to, for example, run a dishwasher, dryer, and heating all at once than if you plan to use only one of these systems at a time.

3. How long do you need to rely upon battery energy? This will depend on climate factors. If, for example, you live in a place that has sun nearly every day, you may need less battery capacity for your solar energy system than if you live in a place that has a "dry season" and you rely upon hydro energy.

4. How much installation space do you have? Most home battery systems are moderate in size—the largest is approximately the size of a chest freezer—but you will need a cool, dark space to house the electric system.

You should also consider the battery's depth of discharge (or DoD), which describes the percent of the battery's capacity that can be used without reducing its lifespan. Aim for one that has 90% or more DoD.

BACKUP ENERGY GENERATION

Another system to ensure that you have energy even when your primary off-grid system isn't functioning at its peak capacity is having a backup energy generator. These systems are less efficient than home batteries, as they often run on gasoline, diesel, or other non-renewable resources. They have, however, a lower up-front cost than home battery systems and can provide a third layer of protection for homes that have inadequate home battery systems or for those who just desire extra peace of mind regarding their energy needs.

Gasoline generators are one of the most common backup generator choices due to their low start-up and maintenance costs and the ready availability of fuel (Jackery 2024). They are also frequently portable. Gasoline generators cannot be used in enclosed spaces, however, as they emit fumes that can be dangerous if inhaled. They also have comparatively short lifespans and are not sufficiently strong to power heavy-duty appliances.

Diesel generators have a higher output than gasoline generators (Jackery 2024). They also have a longer lifespan and use fuel more efficiently than gasoline generators. They are also not suitable for indoor use, however, and tend to be more expensive to purchase. They require regular maintenance.

Portable solar generators have lower maintenance costs than gasoline or diesel generators as they run from the sun—just like solar panels that may power your whole house. You can make your own solar generator by attaching small solar panels, a converter, and a battery to a handheld cart, which will then let your renewable energy source go wherever you go (Practical Survivalist 2018). Portable solar generators have the same limitations as solar power does overall; however, when the sun isn't shining, they will produce energy at a much lower rate than on a sunny day, and they won't draw in energy at night.

In a long-term emergency, having adequate food, shelter, water, and energy may make you the subject of intrigue by those around you who are less well-prepared for what the world has to throw at you. Similarly, widespread emergencies can leave healthcare systems overburdened or unavailable. In the next chapter, we'll discuss how to safeguard your home and family so that you are secure even when external help is limited.

7
CHAPTER SEVEN—S:
STAY SAFE

The National Safety Council estimates that 86% of all preventable injury-related deaths are caused by three things: motor vehicle accidents or misuse, poisoning, and falls. Falls also account for 35% of all preventable nonfatal injuries (NSC 2022). Preventable injuries, meanwhile, are the third most common cause of death in the United States, following heart disease and cancer.

What this means is that staying safe is, more than anything else, a matter of preventing accidents and knowing how to treat them when they prove unavoidable. In this chapter, we'll discuss broad safety protocols including first aid for various injury scenarios, how to call for help when at-home medicine is insufficient, and how to protect yourself and your home from aggressors.

FIRST THINGS FIRST...FIRST AID

There are certain first aid skills that everyone should know, though these skills become even more important when living off the grid, as it may be difficult or impossible to seek a doctor's aid in a timely manner. We'll cover several core situations and how to handle them so that you can aid yourself or a family member in the case of distress.

Nosebleed

Most nosebleeds can be treated at home. To stop a nosebleed (NHS 2024):

1. Sit down, lean forward, and pinch the soft part of your nose above your nostrils for ten to fifteen minutes. (Note that while conventional wisdom suggested tilting your head backward, this is not the recommended position per medical sources).

2. Breathe through your mouth. Spit out any blood that enters your throat or mouth. Do not swallow blood.

3. Put an ice pack on your forehead or the back of your neck.

Nosebleeds will typically resolve after this treatment, but you should seek medical help if you take a blood thinner, have heart palpitations or shortness of breath, or have a clotting disorder.

CPR

Cardiopulmonary resuscitation, or CPR, can keep blood circulating after someone's heart stops beating or is beating inefficiently. To administer CPR to an adult ("CPR Steps" n.d.):

1. Check for responsiveness, breathing, or serious bleeding. Staunch any bleeding as well as possible. Check to ensure that the airway is clear of any physical obstacles.

2. Place the person on their back on a flat, firm surface and kneel beside them. Center your two hands on their chest, lock your elbows, and hold your shoulders directly over your hands. Compress at least two inches at a rate of 100-120 compressions per minute. Allow the chest to return to its normal position after each compression.

3. Compress thirty times, then give two breaths by tilting the person's chin, pinching their nose shut, and making a complete seal over their mouth with your mouth. Breathe into their mouth for one second, then allow air to exit before giving the second breath. If the breath does not cause their chest to rise, check the seal of your

mouth and ensure that nothing is blocking the airway. Pause to see if the person has resumed breathing on their own.

4. Repeat in cycles of thirty compressions and two breaths. The gaps between compression sets should not be longer than ten seconds.

To administer CPR to an infant or small child ("Child and Baby CPR" n.d.):

1. Check the child or baby for responsiveness, breathing, or serious bleeding. Staunch any bleeding as well as possible. Check to ensure that the airway is clear of physical obstacles.

2. Place the person on their back on a flat, firm surface. For a child, kneel beside them. Position your arms straight, your shoulders, and locked elbows directly over your hands. Place hands with fingers interlaced, one atop the other, at the center of the child's chest. For a small child, you may use just one hand. For a baby, stand or kneel to the side, keeping your hips at a slight angle. Place both thumbs side by side at the center of the baby's chest, below the nipple line. Use your other fingers to provide support to the baby's back. For both ages, compress at a rate of 100-120 compressions per minute in sets of thirty. Compress two inches for children and 1.5 inches for babies, allowing the chest to return to normal between compressions.

3. Follow the same breathing pattern as in adult CPR. Repeat cycles as needed.

Always call for medical help as soon as possible when performing CPR. If phone lines are usable, call 911 before beginning compressions. Use an AED (or defibrillator) as soon as possible.

Choking

Choking is most common in small children, but signs of gagging can often be mistaken for choking. If a child is coughing, talking, or making loud gagging sounds, they are not choking. If their gagging is silent or accompanied by a high-pitched noise, your child is choking. To help a choking child or adult (Stanford Medicine n.d.):

1. Stand behind the choking person and wrap your arms around their waist.

2. Make a fist and place it, with the thumb facing in, below the chest and above the navel.

3. Grab your fist with your other hand and press into the abdomen with a quick upward push. Repeat the inward and upward thrust until the object comes out of the person's mouth.

If an infant is choking (Stanford Medicine n.d.):

1. Put the baby face-down on your forearm. Rest your arm on your thigh. With the heel of your other hand, give five quick, forceful blows between the shoulder blades.

2. If this fails, turn the child on their back so their head is lower than their chest. Place two fingers on the center of the breastbone below the nipple line. Press inward rapidly five times.

3. Alternate back blows and front presses until the object comes out.

When someone chokes, you should seek medical attention immediately. If phone lines are active, call 911. Even if the object comes out, particles may have entered the lungs, which can cause serious health concerns.

Setting a Splint

Splints immobilize an injured body part to prevent further damage. Makeshift splints can provide much-needed support to minor injuries like sprains and strains. They can also stabilize major injuries, like fractures or broken bones, while you wait for more extensive medical care. To apply a splint (SJAA 2022):

1. Find a suitable object. Seek something long enough to extend past both ends of the injured body part, wide enough to support the injury, and as firm and straight as possible. Possibilities include a length of wood, tree limbs, or rolled newspapers. For leg or finger injuries, you can use the uninjured limb to provide support to the injured one.

2. Check for other injuries if there is an open wound, staunch the bleeding as much as possible.

3. Pad the splint. Attach the splint to the injured limb by gently wrapping bandages around the natural hollows of the limb. Wrap them tight enough that you cannot insert multiple fingers underneath the bandage but not so tight that you cause the skin to bulge around the bandage, as this can compromise circulation.

4. For a leg injury, make sure you also wrap the foot and ankle.

Most injuries that require splints also require medical assistance, though, in the case of minor injuries, this may not be an emergency that requires calling 911.

Stopping Bleeding

Bleeding has an enormous range of severity, from very minor to life-threatening. Some bleeding requires medical attention, such as if caused by a jagged or deep wound or comes from an animal bite. If an object is embedded in the body, don't remove it; this can make bleeding worse. If bleeding does not stop after approximately twenty minutes of first aid, seek medical attention.

Whether you are managing a small cut on your own or waiting for more experienced medical personnel to arrive, treat bleeding (Hepler 2018):

1. Have the person sit or lie down so that you can elevate the bleeding limb above the heart.

2. Remove obvious debris. If the cut is small, wash it with soap and water.

3. Apply pressure with a sterile cloth or bandage for about ten minutes. If blood soaks through, add another cloth and apply pressure for a further ten minutes.

4. When bleeding stops, apply a clean adhesive or cloth bandage.

Treating Burns

First-degree burns, which only affect the top layer of skin, can be treated at home. If your skin blisters, this is a second-degree burn—if it is very small (about one to two inches or smaller), you can treat it like you do a first-degree burn. Any larger, and you need medical assistance. Third-degree burns, when your skin appears burned or charred, require immediate medical assistance, even if they do not hurt. This just means the nerve endings have been destroyed (JHM n.d.).

To treat a first-degree or very minor second-degree burn (AAD n.d.):

1. Cool the burn by immersing it in cool tap water or applying cool, wet compresses for about ten minutes. This should cause the pain to subside. Avoid very cold water.

2. Apply petroleum jelly two or three times per day while the burn heals. Avoid ointments, topical antibiotics, or butter (an old home remedy that may contribute to infection).

3. Cover the burn with a non-stick sterile bandage. Do not pop any blisters that form.

4. Protect from the sun until the burn is fully healed.

Identifying Concussions

A concussion is a mild brain injury caused by an impact on the head. Though concussions are less severe than traumatic brain injuries (TBIs), they still should be treated as potentially serious injuries. Signs of concussion following a brain injury include (UC Davis Health 2022):

- Blurred or double vision
- Unusual pupil size
- Trouble focusing
- Confusion
- Eye strain
- Light sensitivity
- Loss of consciousness

Seek medical attention for a concussion if you lose consciousness, have a headache that is severe, long-lasting, or worsens over time, have trouble waking up, vomit, feel weak or numb, struggle to walk or talk, or have a seizure. Mild concussions will typically resolve after resting for several days; failing to rest can worsen the injury. If symptoms persist for weeks, this may be a sign of a TBI, which can have diverse and far-reaching medical implications.

Poisoning

Most poisonings happen when someone accidentally swallows, injects, or inhales a harmful substance. Because poisoning can happen in many different ways, ingesting a toxic substance can also have many different symptoms. If you think someone has been poisoned, check for chemical-smelling breath, burns around the mouth, vomiting, unusual odors, or difficulty breathing. Examine the area for potential poisons that the person may have ingested. In the case of suspected poisoning, call 911 immediately (Mount Sinai n.d.).

Do not induce vomiting in someone who may have been poisoned unless directed to do so by poison control. If they vomit and it is possible to save the vomit, do so; if they have been poisoned by a plant, this can help identify the toxin and thus the treatment. Remove any clothing that has touched the poison. Open windows and doors to protect against fumes. Flush the skin with water where the substance has touched the skin.

Identifying Strokes

Strokes see the highest rates of recovery when they are treated immediately. Call 911 if you see signs of stroke, including (AHA n.d.):

- Facial drooping
- Arm weakness
- Speech difficulty
- Numbness, particularly on one side of the body
- Confusion
- Dizziness, or loss of balance or coordination
- Trouble seeing from one or both eyes
- Severe headache without a cause

ASSEMBLING A FIRST AID KIT

Having a robust first aid kit is a necessary component for off-grid living. You should have a first aid kit at home, in your car, and anywhere you spend considerable time (such as at work, in a workshop, etc.). Many first aid kits are commercially available, but building your own kit will let you make a kit that is better stocked for less money. It will also help familiarize you with everything in the kit, which will make it easier to use in an emergency.

Your first aid kit (or kits if you are building at-home and on-the-go options) should be sturdy, waterproof, and clearly labeled. The list below will help you build a complete first aid kit and reduce contents as desired for smaller kits that you intend to make portable.

First aid basics:

- Absorbent compresses
- Adhesive bandages (various sizes)
- Adhesive cloth tape
- Aloe vera gel
- Antibiotic ointment
- Antiseptic wipes
- Blister tape
- Breathing barrier (for CPR)
- Burn cream
- Butterfly closures
- Cold compresses
- Cotton swabs
- Emergency blanket
- Gauze pads (various sizes)
- Gauze roll
- Hand sanitizer
- Heat packs
- Hydrocortisone ointment

- Insect repellant
- Non-latex gloves
- Oral thermometer
- Roller bandage
- Scissors
- Splints
- Sunscreen
- Tourniquet
- Triangular bandage (or sling)
- Tweezers

Medications:

- Antidiarrheals
- Antihistamines
- Antacid
- Epinephrine auto-injector (like EpiPen)
- Glucose tablets
- Oral analgesics (such as ibuprofen or acetaminophen)
- Oral antibiotics (such as doxycycline or ampicillin)
- Prescription medications that you use regularly
- Rehydration electrolytes
- Topical analgesics

Non-medical items:

- Paper to record medical information
- Pens and pencils
- Permanent marker (to write on bandages as needed)
- Safety pins
- Trash bags (for sanitary disposal)
- Ziploc bags (for sanitary, secure storage)

Once you have built the first aid kits you need, ensure that you can quickly access each kit and that you know how to use all the equipment inside. Check the expiration dates on all the medications inside at least twice per year to ensure that they haven't expired. If your kit is exposed to fluctuations in temperature (if you, for example, keep it in your car), periodically check to ensure that nothing has been damaged, melted, or frozen.

NATURAL AND HOME REMEDIES

In off-grid situations, conventional or modern medicine is not always available. Restocking these medications may also prove difficult in crisis scenarios. Supplementing your first aid kit and medicine cabinet with natural and home remedies can help keep your treatments renewable. Consider including the following medicinal herbs and natural remedies in your home medicine practice.

Chamomile

Chamomile can be used to help with anxiety, promote relaxation, heal wounds, and reduce inflammation and swelling. Use the plant's flower to achieve its desired effects; you can steep the flowers (fresh or dried) into a tea or use it as a compress. Note that chamomile may make you feel tired, particularly if combined with other medications (URMC n.d.).

Echinacea

Studies indicate that echinacea can help with upper respiratory infections, while folk wisdom indicates that using the leaf, stalk, or roots of the plant can help to treat or prevent colds. Note that if you are allergic to ragweed, you may also have an allergic reaction to echinacea (URMC n.d.).

Honeysuckle

Blending honeysuckle leaves with water, then straining out the leaves debris to make a "juice," will relieve discomfort from poison ivy and may provide a soothing sensation for other skin irritants (Emergency Essentials 2014).

Ginger

Ginger can ease nausea caused by pregnancy, motion sickness, or chemotherapy. Ongoing research indicates that ginger may have anti-cancer agents and is a strong anti-inflammatory and antioxidant. Ginger can be eaten raw, brewed into tea, or added to food (URMC n.d.).

Mud

Mud, when applied to the skin and left to dry before removal, can help draw out bee stingers and venom, relieve the itch caused by insect bites, and soothe stinging nettle rashes (Emergency Essentials 2014).

Tea Tree Oil

Tea tree oil is an anti-inflammatory substance that can help treat infections caused by bacteria or fungi. It is also a popular treatment for acne, though it should be used sparingly, as some find that it dries the skin excessively (Van Sloun 2015).

Vinegar

Heating vinegar and inhaling the vapor with a towel draped over your head (to keep the steam close to you) can help clear sinus congestion. Vinegar, when mixed with water in a one-to-one ratio, can create a mild antibacterial cleanser that is safe to use on surfaces that will later touch food (Emergency Essentials 2014).

SELF-DEFENSE BASICS

Physical threats may increase in a crisis, particularly when others feel frightened and ill-prepared to adjust to new emergencies. Before you enter a physical alteration, however, seek to prevent a fight in the first place. Trust your instincts when you suspect a situation will become unsafe and project confidence, as this will discourage some would-be assailants from attack. Most attackers seek victims that seem vulnerable, so making yourself an inaccessible target and setting strong verbal boundaries will dissuade some attackers.

When a physical altercation is unavoidable, use simple techniques to defend yourself long enough to get away. Use your elbows to strike at your assailant's face; this versatile move can be done when you are facing the attacker or when they have seized you from behind, and your elbow can often be used with greater force than your fist (Davis 2018). If an attacker is approaching, you can use your dominant leg to kick them in the groin; this move is more effective against men than women. If they get too close for your foot to be effective, thrust your knee up and into their groin (Davis 2018).

The most effective strategy for self-defense beginners is to run away as soon as you are free from an assailant's grasp. Doing so while they are incapacitated from a blow will help you get a head start if they try to pursue you, though many attackers will not give chase as they seek a vulnerable, easy victim.

EMERGENCY SIGNAL CRAFTING

If you get lost away from civilization and are unable to return on your own, such as if you are injured, you may need to signal for help. Consider the following methods to help draw aid to your location in a crisis.

Signal Fire

A signal fire is likely the most well-known emergency signal, and for good reason; a large signal fire can send up a large plume of smoke that can rise above other obstacles that block you from view, creating a sign that is visible for miles. To build a natural signal fire, build a teepee-shaped fire, starting with dry wood and kindling. Once the fire is burning steadily, add green foliage to create the visible, billowing smoke that will constitute your signal. Be sure not to build a natural signal fire in any place where you could cause a larger, more dangerous fire that you cannot control (Castillon 2024).

If you have a flare with you, this can create a larger, long-burning flame that can be waved like a beacon when attached to a long stick (James 2020).

Reflective Signal

The flash of light from a mirror can travel up to ten miles, making it one of the farthest-reaching non-electronic help signals (James 2020). Carrying a mirror is an easy add to your hiking pack, and you can improvise a reflective signal with the screen of your cell phone in a pinch—though it will not work as well or send as far a signal as will a mirror.

Whistle

A whistle is the unsung hero of emergency signals. Though simple, whistles have considerable advantages—they're small, cheap, easy to attach to multiple pieces of equipment, and usable even if you are too injured to build a fire or wave a reflective signal. Keep some in different locations and wear one around your neck when you are hiking. Use three sharp blasts to signify distress—something that will garner attention even if it's night or you are located somewhere that has low visibility, such as if you've fallen into a hole (James 2020).

KEEPING YOUR OFF-GRID HOUSE SECURE

In crisis scenarios, emergency response teams can be unreliable, as they may be focused on other things than keeping your personal property secure. To keep your home and land safe while living off the grid, consider the following safety measures (Peterson 2024):

1. Solar-powered security cameras and motion-activated lighting
2. Strong fencing
3. Guard dogs
4. Neighborhood watch

These strategies are all either low- or no-energy and can run on power sources that are reliable even when power grids are down. Any alarm and lighting systems should be regularly inspected to ensure that their solar batteries are intact and holding a charge. Physical barriers like fencing, reinforced points of entry, or railings that cover windows should be subject to frequent visual and touch-based inspections. Keep a record of your inspections so that you can chart any changes over time. If you use systems that require inputting a code, avoid making the code something easy to guess (like a significant date) and update it regularly.

If thieves do access your home, it will be difficult for them to obtain anything of value. Use clever hiding places like the freezer (in a Ziploc bag beneath the ice), the pantry (inside a canister of flour or coffee), or the back of pieces of furniture (secured with tape) to hide valuable documents, any stashes of cash that you keep on hand, or non-currency sources of money, such as gold or jewelry.

Fire Safety

As with injuries, most things that compromise your home arise due to accidents, not malice. A house fire is one of the home accidents that can have the most devastating consequences, including physical injury, loss of possessions, and the destruction of your home. Proper home fire safety includes knowing what to do before and during a fire.

Before a Fire

To prevent a fire from sparking, employ strategies such as (Bluetti 2023):

- Unplug electrical devices that are not in use.
- Regularly inspect electrical and heating systems for any damage. If you have a wood-burning fireplace, ensure that this is checked before lighting any fires.
- Don't leave any candles, ovens, or cigarettes burning unattended. Avoid smoking in the house.
- Teach fire safety measures to children who might grow curious about how matches or lighters work.

You should also rehearse your fire evacuation plan (as detailed in Chapter One) to ensure that your family is prepared in the event of a fire. Check batteries on smoke detectors regularly and keep fire extinguishers in several locations in your home, such as in the kitchen, garage, or basement. These should be easily accessible and kept close to places where fires are more likely to spark.

During a Fire

If a fire breaks out in your home, extinguish it quickly, if possible, using the following methods (LS Fire Group 2021):

- **Class A fires** occur when solid materials like paper, fabric, or wood ignite. Use water extinguishers to put out this fire.
- **Class B fires** occur when a flammable liquid like alcohol or fuel is ignited. These fires must be extinguished with a foam extinguisher that smothers the flames. Water can spread flammable liquids and thus cannot be used to extinguish these fires.
- **Class C fires** occur when flammable gases ignite. These fires are particularly dangerous as they can cause explosions. To suppress class C fires, switch off the gas supply and use a dry powder fire extinguisher.
- **Class D fires** occur when combustible metals, such as powdered metals or shavings, accumulate and ignite. These are less common in home settings. Class D fires must be extinguished with a dry powder extinguisher.
- **Class F fires** occur when cooking oil ignites. These are common in kitchens. Like with class B fires, water can cause these fires to spread, so you must extinguish them by using a wet chemical fire extinguisher or smothering the flames.
- **Electrical fires** occur when overloaded or faulty electrical components ignite. To suppress these fires, turn off the electricity source and use a dry powder extinguisher.

If you cannot extinguish a fire, crawl beneath the smoke to escape and run to safety (McEntire and Bradford 2024). Check doors for signs of fire before opening them; practice this as part of your fire evacuation procedures.

We have now covered all the basics necessary to establish your life off the grid. Life, however, isn't just about surviving—it is about having meaning and purpose to your daily experiences. In the next chapter, we'll discuss how to build productive daily habits that lead to growth, long-term resilience, and self-reliance.

8

CHAPTER EIGHT—T: THRIVE... DON'T JUST SURVIVE

T he Greek poet Archilochus is reported to have said, "We don't rise to the level of our expectations; we fall to the level of our training."

While scholars have debated the true origin of this quote, which was supposedly uttered nearly two thousand years ago, its lesson is undeniable. You will always be better equipped to face something you have trained to handle than something you have not.

In this chapter, we'll approach strategies for cultivating a tactical mindset, practicing proven survival techniques, and building habits that ensure that you're prepared to handle any challenges that come your way while living off the grid.

SHARPENING YOUR SURVIVAL SKILLS

Survival relies on many different kinds of strength: physical strength, mental strength, and emotional strength. Building each of these takes practice, dedication, and foresight—you cannot expect this strength to simply materialize when needed if you have not culti-vated it. The following sections will explore strategies to promote

your physical, mental, and spiritual fitness so that you have the fortitude to face any disaster.

Strengthening Your Body

Strength and fitness training for preparedness is not about
looking good in a certain outfit; it's about knowing that you have the
physical ability to perform whatever task is needed, whether that
means carrying heavy weights for long distances or protecting yourself against natural and manmade threats.

Consider the following strength-building exercises, all of which
can be done without extensive gym equipment, making them ideal
for off-grid living (Canadian Prepper 2021):

- Squats—this exercise works your quadriceps, glutes,
  core, and calves, and can be done with no equipment. To
  practice a squat, bend until your knees are at a 90-degree
  angle, keeping your core tight and as upright as possible.
  To increase the difficulty, you can hold a weight (such as
  a kettlebell or heavy household object) with your arms
  halfway extended in front of you.
- Pushups and planks—these exercises work your core,
  shoulders, and back. To complete, face the ground with
  your arms fully extended, directly beneath your
  shoulders, holding your back in a straight line from toes
  to head. Holding this position is a plank; bending your
  arms to 90 degrees and back straight again is a push up.
  Increase sets each day as your strength grows.
- Yoga—while these body-weight postures aren't always
  the first to come to mind when you think of building
  strength, yoga can help your muscles learn new
  positions, strengthen lesser-used muscle groups, and
  take you through stretches that protect you while you
  strength train.
- Functional training—doing the things that you will need
  to do in a survival situation is a great way to double up

your strength training with practice for different crises. Try going for long hikes carrying heavy packs, carrying five to seven gallons of water for a mile, or carrying a member of your family as if they are injured (Laws and Chymiy 2018).

Establishing a fitness routine depends on making reasonable changes and setting realistic goals. It is much easier, for example, to get disheartened if you set (and inevitably miss) an unattainable goal than if you set smaller, incremental goals that you can gradually meet. A recommended minimum exercise program is 150 minutes per week (Semeco 2023); set a schedule to start that works with your life, including rest days. If you are a beginner, you may need to add more rest than you planned to avoid injury. As your strength increases, you will be able to exercise more reliably without risking harm.

Find activities that feel rewarding for you, whether because you enjoy them on your own or because you find the results worth the effort. Choosing an activity that you hate makes you far more likely to give up the routine (Robinson, Segal, and Smith 2018). Exercising with someone else—like a family member or friend—can also help keep you accountable and, therefore, more likely to stick to a routine.

Physical health goes beyond exercising, of course. For your body to function properly when you need it to, it requires adequate rest and fuel. Carbohydrates, fat, and protein are all important for building muscle. The Academy of Nutrition and Dietetics estimates that about half your daily calories should come from carbohydrates, with particular attention to carbs that provide dietary fiber. Note that carbohydrates can come from unexpected sources, such as dairy products (Klemm 2024).

Protein, meanwhile, should make up between ten and thirty-five percent of your total daily calories—a contrast to conventional wisdom that insists that more is better when it comes to protein and muscle-building. Estimate nine ounces per day of protein foods, including fish, beans, meat, or low-fat dairy (Klemm 2024). Fat should account for approximately twenty to thirty-five percent of your daily calories; these should consist primarily of heart-healthy fats, including vegetable oils and fats from nuts or fish (Klemm 2024).

Proper sleep is another key facet in physical health; research indicates that insufficient or poor sleep contributes to mental illness, dangerous accidents, diabetes, and heart disease (Chattu et al. 2018). Maintaining poor sleep habits, also known as sleep hygiene, can therefore provide a significant detriment to your health and overall quality of life.

Implement good sleep habits like keeping consistent sleep and wake times, seeking light exposure during the day, and avoiding it at night (especially blue light, like from your cell phone or other devices). Limit alcohol and caffeine consumption and keep any caffeine to early in the day (Mawer 2024). If you frequently wake in the night to urinate, drink water earlier in the day so that you can remain hydrated without compromising your sleep schedule.

Having a regular exercise routine (although not right before bed, as exercise can energize you) and balanced nutritional habits can also improve your sleep (Mawer 2024). This means that physical health arises from a series of overlapping qualities, each of which reinforce the others to maximize your overall fitness.

STRENGTHENING YOUR BRAIN

Knowledge is power in a survival situation; knowing how to do something can mean the difference between life and death when facing a sudden disaster. That said, suddenly implementing many new skills all at once can be mentally draining—think back, for example, to learning to drive a car. Your first time behind the wheel likely took far more focus and mental energy than it does after putting years and miles under your belt.

Similarly, establishing certain habits *before* they're needed means that they will take up less of your mental load when they become a matter of necessity. Add the following habits to your daily routine so that when disaster strikes, you will be ready.

Keep Material Necessities on Hand

When living on the grid, it's relatively easy to access material necessities. Depending on where you live, a grocery store, gas station, and bank are probably within a short drive. When systems collapse, however, these necessities may suddenly become nearly impossible to access—and all the more valuable for it.

Make it a habit to always keep the following things on hand (Coonradt 2020):

- An everyday carry (or EDC) kit of the things you use almost every day. This might include your phone, a pocket knife, a flashlight, a wallet, pens and paper, or other common objects. Consider having alternate kits for different daily needs (for example, for workdays or weekends).
- A half-full tank of gas (at minimum) on every vehicle. Then you will know you have fuel in case you need to quickly evacuate.
- Cell phone chargers—and maintain at least a 50% charge on your phone at all times.
- Cash. If electronic payment systems fail, using cash will be your primary method of currency. Focus on smaller bills, as you may not be able to make change from large bills in an emergency.

Build a Bug Out Bag

A "bug out bag" contains all the things that are not day-to-day necessities in non-survival situations, but which become necessities when things go wrong. A good bug-out bag should be something that you can carry for miles (practicing with this bag is a good thing to include in your fitness routine) and that contains all your survival necessities.

Choose multi-purpose gear when building your bug-out bag, as this will let you minimize space and weight while retaining the maximum utility of your pack's contents. When building your bag, consider adding (Ruiz 2013):

- A survival hatchet, which often works as a hatchet, shovel, wrench, and pry tool
- A multitool, such as a Swiss Army knife
- A tarp, which can, as we discussed in our chapter on shelters, be used to protect you from the elements in many ways
- Plastic bags, which can keep tinder and matches dry, keep first aid items sanitary, and keep small items contained so you can find them more easily
- Duct tape
- Paracord, which can also help build shelters with greater structural integrity

Buy Extra Groceries

Make it a part of your regular grocery habit to purchase one or two items for your emergency food and water storage. This can help defray the costs of stocking emergency rations (and household supplies like soap and medication) all at once and can help you make sure that you replace supplies at regular intervals. If you replace shelf-stable items before they expire, they also don't go to waste; you can just put the new bag of flour, for example, in place of the one that has been in storage and use up the old. You can also save money by stocking up on freezer and pantry items when they happen to be on sale.

Practice Situational Awareness

Make it a habit to continually track what happens around you. This includes things like (Coonradt 2020):

- Knowing your usual surroundings well. People lose their cool in an emergency, but knowing safe alternate exits and places to hide, when necessary, can help you remain calm.
- Assessing the current level of danger. Use your instincts *and* your senses to tell if you could easily escape your situation if something dangerous suddenly happened and to assess whether something is likely to become dangerous. Ask if there are any unusual people where they shouldn't be or if any environmental threats are likely to be nearby. Practice making these assessments until they become instinctual.
- Locating multiple exits whenever you arrive in a new location.
- Reducing obstacles between yourself and a potential avenue of exit.

Continue Learning and Reading

Though you have gathered many necessary skills by reading this far in this book, don't let your survival education end when you reach the final page. Reading different sources can offer ongoing information in a variety of formats and on endless topics. Read news articles, how-to's, and memoirs of people who have successfully lived off the grid for extended periods of time. This will keep you appraised of current events (which can help you predict the likelihood of imminent disaster), will stimulate your mind, and will help you add new skills to your arsenal.

Learn How to Start a Fire

Starting a fire without matches or a lighter is a laborious skill but one that grows easier as you practice. Rehearsing the skill before you are staking your life on it increases your potential survival exponentially.

The first step to starting a fire is accessing timber or material that ignites easily to turn a spark or ember into a flame. You can make your own tinder and carry it with you (such as cotton balls dipped in Vaseline, which will ignite quickly and burn for a while) or find it in the wild. Good sources of tinder include dry grass, animal nests, pine tree sap, tree bark, or any "downy" plant material (Mileham 2022). Alcohol wipes and hand sanitizer also ignite well and may already be present in your backpack when needed.

The following are basic methods for starting fires without modern equipment.

Hand Drill

The hand drill method is one of the most difficult ways to start a fire, but it requires the least materials. To use this method ("Start a Fire Without Matches" 2021):

1. Build a tinder nest.

2. Cut a V-shaped notch in the fireboard and make a small depression next to it.

3. Place bark underneath the notch.

4. Place a spindle (a stick about two feet long and as straight as possible) into the depression. Roll the spindle between your hands, keeping pressure on the board. Continue until an ember forms on the fireboard.

5. When the ember forms, tap the fireboard to drop it onto the bark, transfer it to the tinder, blow on the ember gently until the tinder ignites, and build your fire.

Flint and Steel

Making a fire with flint and steel is far easier than building a fire from wood friction alone, but it does require you to have the necessary materials in advance. Flint and steel are reusable; however, unlike matches, they do not require filling up on fluid, like lighters. To make a fire with flint and steel (Eureka! 2015):

1. Build a tinder nest.

2. Strike the flint with the steel striker to generate sparks. Angle the sparks and continue striking until they land on the tinder.

3. Blow gently on the sparks until they ignite and build your fire.

Batteries and Steel Wool

To build a fire with batteries and steel wool ("Start a Fire Without Matches" 2021):

1. Build a tinder nest.

2. Stretch your steel wool until it is about six inches long and half an inch wide.

3. Hold the wool in one hand and rub the battery's contact points on the wool. (A 9-volt battery works best.)

4. When the wool begins to glow and burn, blow on it gently and quickly transfer it to the tinder nest, as it will not remain lit for very long.

Learn How to Maintain a Fire

Once you've built your hard-won fire, you want to keep it from going out. To keep your fire burning as long as possible (Berard 2023):

- Use dry wood whenever possible. Damp wood will create extra smoke and will struggle to ignite.
- Structure your fire with smaller logs and dry kindling at the bottom with larger logs on top, leaving space between each log. This will create the proper airflow to keep your fire burning.
- Choose hardwood, when available, as it will burn longer and provide more heat than softer woods, like pine.
- Remove excess ash, as this can smother flames. Leave a small amount of ash to insulate coals, thus retaining heat.
- Add additional fuel gradually to promote longevity; overloading a fire pit can cause wood to burn more quickly and then die down quickly.

Learn Navigation Basics

In a true off-grid situation, you won't be able to rely on GPS systems to help navigate. To ensure that you will still be able to get where you're going without technological help, learn to use a compass and a map to navigate.

Using a Compass

The process for orienting yourself using a compass can be remembered using ABC (Joque and Wowk 2022):

A: **Align** the compass

B: Read the **bearing**

C: Set a **course**

To align your compass, turn the compass housing until the red magnetic needle (which points to the magnetic north) is aligned with the red-orienting arrow. Your compass will then be facing magnetic north, which will let you see which direction corresponds to which point on the compass rose.

Next, you will take a bearing or find the direction you want to go based on where you are located. To do so, hold your compass parallel to the ground and point the travel arrow (the arrow that points from the compass' baseplate) toward a landmark, such as a boulder or tree. Then, turn the housing until the compass is aligned. The degree number that lines up with your travel arrow is your bearing. If this measures 90 degrees, for example, your landmark is east of your current point. Use this bearing to know which direction you should travel.

Reading a Map

To begin navigating using a map, first learn map symbols and what different colors mean on the map you are using. Most maps will have a key that helps indicate what you are seeing, but getting accustomed to these symbols can help prevent you from getting overwhelmed when looking at the (often visually busy) map.

To use the map to set your course, you will have to take a bearing from a map and from your current location. To take a bearing from the map (Joque and Wowk 2022):

1. Lay the edge of your compass base plate (which runs parallel to the travel arrow) on the map, running from your location to your destination.

2.Hold the base plate so it does not move. Rotate the compass housing until the compass-orienting arrow (not the magnetic needle, which you do not need at this point) runs parallel to the vertical grid lines on the map.

3.Read the bearing where the degree dial meets the travel arrow. This is your degree bearing for your direction of travel to your destination.

Once you know what direction you need to travel to reach your destination, use the ABC method to determine which direction has the same degree bearing as the one you read off your map bearing. Regularly read as you go to ensure that you have not deviated from the necessary direction.

Learn to Budget and Barter

It's nearly impossible to predict how a large-scale disaster will affect employment opportunities. To pad your bank account so that you have needed funds even when your earning potential is uncertain, learn to budget and live below your means, which will add up to savings that will be there when necessary. Look for ways to lower discretionary expenses, such as maintaining services that you don't truly need. Shop for groceries in bulk to cut costs or get a roommate or smaller apartment, if possible. You can also negotiate with your service providers to lower bills, something not everyone realizes is possible (Lee 2024).

You can also seek opportunities to barter for goods and services instead of buying everything you need. Even if you feel that you don't have marketable skills, think of nontraditional ways that you can exchange what you have for what you need. If your neighbor is a plumber, for example, he might be willing to fix your sink if you offer to do a couple of hours of childcare. Alternatively, long-term swaps can help maximize the productivity of your homestead and that of your neighbors. If they have a robust vegetable garden and you have more chickens and, therefore, eggs than you can consume, plan to exchange tomatoes for eggs each week. Bartering relationships like this fosters off-grid living without forcing you to do every single thing yourself—or forcing you to implement these changes all at once. Living off the grid doesn't mean living entirely without community, so setting up bartering partnerships with neighbors helps you both make your off-grid lives more sustainable.

Bartering also creates a micro-economy that is less susceptible to the variability of money. The price of a gallon of milk might go up and down each week or month at the grocery store, but if you know you're going to exchange with your neighbor for some time spent helping them fix up their property, you have that deal cemented ahead of time. There's less guessing when it comes to time to make the exchange. You can, of course, renegotiate trades with friends and neighbors—as long as everyone feels that the swap is a fair one, you can consider the bartering successful.

STRENGTHENING YOUR SPIRIT

Adapting to change and thriving even when things go wrong requires physical ability and mental know-how, yes. But it also requires emotional fortitude, which will help you keep fighting for a better life even when things continue to go wrong—and things always do go wrong in an emergency, even when you're well-prepared.

Practicing the appropriate mindset and working on your spiritual health to maintain resilience when disaster strikes can take your off-grid life from a daily slog to something that is truly worth living.

Cultivate a Survival Mindset

Cultivating a survival mindset should not be mistaken for putting a positive spin on things or keeping a smile on your face no matter what. By contrast, this kind of blind optimism can actually prove detrimental to your survival. If you always expect things to go well, you will be unprepared when they don't—and likely disheartened.

Stark pessimism isn't safe, either, however. If you believe things are always going to go poorly, it can be easy to fall into despair, which makes it hard to summon the fortitude to continue fighting for survival.

A survival mindset threads the needle between these two extremes. This mindset accepts that things may be bad but does not necessarily admit that current bad conditions mean perpetual bad conditions. A survival mindset, however, does not predict that things will become good again by a certain date or time, leading to discouragement if that self-imposed deadline is not met. Instead, someone with a survival mindset accepts that something bad is happening and grows determined to face it anyway.

To cultivate your survival mindset, recognize the negative emotions that come with a hard situation. Don't try to deny them. Allow yourself a brief pause to feel those feelings—and then move on. This will keep you focused on moving forward without bogging you down in denial.

Build Resilience

Resilience, or the ability to adapt in the face of significant stress, is not something ingrained that you either have or lack. Instead, resilience is something you can build and strengthen, like a muscle. When it comes to building resilience so that you are more capable of handling stress, trauma, or tragedy, researchers from Yale University suggest (Katella 2022):

1. Practicing acceptance. This means accepting that there are some things that you cannot change or improve and deciding to focus on the things that you can control.

2. Reframing events. This means taking something negative and looking at its positive sides. For example, turning to off-grid living might make some aspects of your life harder. But you can instead choose to focus on how you are developing skills and fostering independence.

3. Building connections. As we've said before, off-grid doesn't mean alone. Find a community that has similar values when it comes to off-grid living and rely upon them to help you through hard times—and ask them to rely upon you in turn.

4. Doing things you enjoy. When you're busy trying to get through a tough time, it can be easy to let your hobbies slide. Pausing to do a pleasurable activity, however, can help recharge you for the struggles that lie ahead. Doing things you enjoy isn't wasting time; it's an investment in your future ability.

5. Making adjustments. Don't stick to a pattern that isn't working. If you are trying to start a garden, become energy-independent, and raise livestock all at once, you might be overburdening yourself. Instead of running yourself ragged, pause and reconsider which of these needs to come first—and then let the others come later when you're better prepared to handle them.

Once you master the habits we've discussed in this chapter, you will find that living off the grid isn't just a matter of surviving. You will find yourself able to truly thrive and enjoy the freedom that self-sufficiency offers you. Your abilities and your confidence will grow hand in hand, which will leave you ready and willing to face whatever the world throws at your feet.

As we reach the end of our book, take a moment to consider all that you have already learned—and then consider what you still wish to learn. This desire for more knowledge will help you keep you moving along your journey toward self-reliance so that the contents of this book become more than just theoretical practices and transform into your daily way of living.

AFTERWORD

If I had said that I feel peace when I watch the news these days, I wouldn't have been telling the truth. The fact of the matter is that the world remains unpredictable, chaotic, strange. Each time I turn on the television, glance at my phone, or read the newspaper, it seems that there's something new and horrible happening somewhere in the world. I still feel the full impact of that uncertainty and danger.

But I no longer feel that lurking sense of unease that I did before I started actively planning how I would survive different disasters. I no longer feel helpless, totally at the mercy of the big, bad world. Now, when I see that there's another massive storm brewing, or the risk of another deadly pathogen on the horizon, I don't panic. I think about the OUTLAST metric and know that I and my family will be ready to survive the next challenge that the world sends our way.

Getting to this point wasn't easy. It took a lot of work and a lot of learning. I still try to learn more about surviving, living independently, and building resilience whenever I can. If the contents of this book seem daunting, know that you are not alone in feeling this way. Motivating others in your orbit to build self-reliance skills can be twice as hard. I remember my brother's reaction when I first encouraged him to actually do something about his fear of the unknown future.

However, inactivity gets you nowhere. If you let that daunting feeling stop you, you'll never feel more secure. If you start making changes and embrace the hard work of getting your home and life disaster-ready, you will find that this work pays dividends when it comes to peace of mind.

I even got my brother to agree that he was right to listen to me, and now we have a vegetable swap that keeps our pantries stocked with twice as much variety as we could generate alone. He has passed along his information, as well, and has brought his in-laws into the off-grid fold. With each step that my loved ones take to build their fortitude and independence, the more I feel secure about our futures and the more confident I grow that learning all these skills was the best decision I've made in a long time.

So, don't wait to see what is going to happen next. Begin preparing today, whether that means stocking your home with emergency preparedness materials, learning to build a shelter in various circumstances, or becoming a sustainable homestead with your own garden, livestock, and energy and water supplies. Starting with a small first step is still starting. Explore for yourself how it is possible to be confident and secure that you can thrive no matter the circumstances—it's a reassuring feeling, one that is worth earning. Your journey toward complete self-reliance begins now.

Thank you for coming along on this journey with me. I hope you now feel as though you have a workable plan for moving toward off-grid living. If you learned something from this book or feel more prepared for emergencies, please consider writing a review. Your feedback helps me reach more audiences, who will, in turn, learn all they need to begin their survival preparations.

YOU CAN HELP OTHERS FEEL THE WONDER OF SELF-SUFFICIENCY

In a world in which the minute small disasters strike, supplies become depleted, and supermarkets are a battleground, it must feel amazing to know what you need to start preparing so that disasters never take you by surprise. You have discovered so many skills that can stand you in good stead right now—even when you are fully on-grid and your daily needs are easily accessible.

From growing your own vegetables and honing techniques such as companion planting and crop rotation to raising chickens and a host of additional animals, you know that even in the worst-case scenario, you'll never go hungry. You know how to source produce and meat *and* how to store, preserve, and process it so that your supplies last for weeks, months, or even years. I hope you are excited about getting your hands on essential equipment, building structures, and starting your first edible garden. I know all this will keep you busy, but before you go, please take just half a minute to leave a quick review of this book.

LEAVE A REVIEW!

Thanks so much for joining me on this journey. My greatest joy is to think of you, the reader, building and growing a community of smart, prepared, self-sufficient people who support and care for each other.

BIBLIOGRAPHY

(AAD), American Academy of Dermatology, n.d. "How to Treat a First-Degree, Minor Burn." Accessed November 19, 2024. https://www.aad.org/public/everyday-care/injured-skin/burns/treat-minor-burns.

(AHA), American Heart Association, n.d. "Stroke Symptoms and Warning Signs." www.stroke.org. Accessed November 19, 2024. https://www.stroke.org/en/about-stroke/stroke-symptoms.

(AHW), American Home Water & Air. 2021. "Multi-Stage Water Filter |," June 15, 2021. https://americanhomewater.com/what-is-a-multi-stage-water-filter/.

American Red Cross, n.d. "Drought Preparedness." Accessed October 23, 2024. https://www.redcross.org/get-help/how-to-prepare-for-emergencies/types-of-emergencies/drought.html.

-------, n.d. "Common Natural Disasters Across US." Accessed October 22, 2024. https://www.redcross.org/get-help/how-to-prepare-for-emergencies/common-natural-disasters-across-us.html.

-------, n.d. "Earthquake Safety." Accessed October 22, 2024. https://www.redcross.org/get-help/how-to-prepare-for-emergencies/types-of-emergencies/earthquake.html

———, n.d. "Home Fire Safety." Accessed October 22, 2024. https://www.redcross.org/get-help/how-to-prepare-for-emergencies/types-of-emergencies/fire.html.

———, n.d. "Hurricane Preparedness." Accessed October 22, 2024. https://www.redcross.org/get-help/how-to-prepare-for-emergencies/types-of-emergencies/hurricane.html.

———, n.d. "Make a First Aid Kit." Accessed November 19, 2024. https://www.redcross.org/get-help/how-to-prepare-for-emergencies/anatomy-of-a-first-aid-kit.html.

———, n.d. "Wildfire Safety." Accessed October 23, 2024. https://www.redcross.org/get-help/how-to-prepare-for-emergencies/types-of-emergencies/wildfire.html.

Bartolone, Ginny. 2022. "How Much Does Boiler Installation and Replacement Cost In 2024?" Forbes Home, August 4, 2022. https://www.forbes.com/home-improvement/hvac/boiler-installation-replacement-cost/.

Beall, Abigail. 2020. "How Long Can You Survive without Water?" BBC, October 19, 2020. https://www.bbc.com/future/article/20201016-why-we-cant-survive-without-water.

Belda, Pascual. n.d. "Solar Water Purifier from Recycled Materials." Indestructables. https://www.instructables.com/Solar-Water-Purifier-From-Recycled-Materials/.

Berard, Michael. 2023. "Tips on How to Keep a Fire Burning Longer." Rocketfire Torch,

September 20, 2023. https://rocketfiretorch.com/blogs/tips-tricks/how-to-keep-a-fire-burning-longer.

Blair, Amanda, and Christina Baker. 2023. "At-Home Hog Slaughter." South Dakota State University Extension, October 23, 2023. https://extension.sdstate.edu/home-hog-slaughter.

Bluetti. 2023. "What to Do Before, During, and After House Fire?" Technology Pioneer in Clean Energy, August 2, 2023. https://www.bluettipower.ph/blogs/news/what-to-do-before-during-and-after-house-fire.

Bradshaw, Tim. 2023. "Off-Grid Water Sources and Options." Off-Grid Rebel, July 31, 2023. https://offgridrebel.com/off-grid-water-sources-and-options/.

Brown, Tom. 1982. "Wilderness Survival Skills: Hunting and Trapping Animals." Mother Earth News, March 1, 1982. https://www.motherearthnews.com/diy/survival-skills-zmaz82mazglo/.

(CADPH), California Department of Public Health. 2017. "When and How to Shelter-in-Place." CA.GOV, April 27, 2017. https://www.cdph.ca.gov/Programs/EPO.

California Childcare Health Program. 2016. "Sample Emergency Disaster Drills." University of California San Francisco (UCSF). https://cchp.ucsf.edu/sites/g/files/tkss-ra181/f/Sample-Emergency-Disaster-Drills.pdf.

Canadian Prepper. 2021."A Prepper's Guide to Strength & Fitness Training for the Apocalypse," May 13, 2021. https://canadianpreparedness.com/blogs/news/a-prepper-s-guide-to-strength-fitness-training-for-the-apocalypse?srsltid=AfmBOorOug-U9Q4kBHTZrmV2cgdVtO3gv1-_FZVbaE6YlPBm5EO_tfc0N.

Canadian Red Cross, n.d. "Preparing Emotionally for Disasters and Emergencies." Accessed October 24, 2024. https://www.redcross.ca/how-we-help/emergencies-and-disasters-in-canada/be-ready-emergency-preparedness-and-recovery/pre-paring-emotionally-for-disasters-and-emergencies.

Castillon, Josh. 2024. "SOS: Get Creative with Emergency Signaling in the Wild." *Outdoor Daddy: Brave the Wild* (blog), February 1, 2024. https://medium.com/@josh.-castillon/sos-get-creative-with-emergency-signaling-in-the-wild-0b2bccd739a2.

(CAWST), Centre for Affordable Water and Sanitation Technology, n.d. "Solar Disinfection (SODIS)." https://www.hwts.info/products-technologies/a01550ee/solar-disin-fection-sodis/technical-information.

(CDC), U.S. Centers for Disease Control. 2021. "Food Preservation: Home Canning Safety | Blogs | CDC," July 19, 2021. https://blogs.cdc.gov/publichealthmat-ters/2021/07/home-canning/.

-------. 2017. "Learn How to Shelter in Place." CDC Emergency Preparedness and You, September 29, 2017. https://emergency.cdc.gov/shelterinplace.asp.

Chambers, Dan. 2021. "15 Edible Survival Plants." Yarden, July 7, 2021. https://www.-yarden.com/blog/15-edible-survival-plants/.

Chattu, Vijay Kumar, Md Dilshad Manzar, Soosanna Kumary, Deepa Burman, David Warren Spence, and Seithikurippu R. Pandi-Perumal. 2018. "The Global Problem of Insufficient Sleep and Its Serious Public Health Implications." *Healthcare (Basel, Switzerland)* 7, no. 1 (December 20, 2018): 1. https://doi.org/10.3390/health-care7010001.

City of Vancouver, n.d. "When to Evacuate or Take Shelter in a Building." Accessed October 29, 2024. https://vancouver.ca/home-property-development/when-to-evacuate-or-take-shelter-in-a-building.aspx.

Coonradt, Coby. 2020. "Habits for Preppers." casualpreppers, September 23, 2020. https://www.casualpreppers.com/single-post/habits-for-preppers.

Coosemans, Sandrine. 2021. "What Are the Best Animals for Self-Sufficiency? - Sunny Simple Living," July 2, 2021. https://sunnysimpleliving.com/best-animals-for-self-sufficiency/.

Cowan, Douglas. 2020. "How to Make a Survival Water Filter." Wilderness Awareness School, March 25, 2020. https://wildernessawareness.org/articles/how-to-make-a-survival-water-filter/.

(CTCN), UN Climate Technology Centre & Network. 2016. "Solar Water Disinfection | Climate Technology Centre & Network." UN Enviornment Programme, November 8, 2016. https://www.ctc-n.org/technologies/solar-water-disinfection.

Davis, Nicole. 2018. "8 Self-Defense Moves Every Woman Should Practice." Healthline, August 29, 2018. https://www.healthline.com/health/womens-health/self-defense-tips-escape.

Dayton, Shane. 2020. "15 Wild Edibles To Save You in the Wild." Secrets of Survival, August 25, 2020. https://secretsofsurvival.com/edible-wild-plants/.

DeGunther, Rick. 2016. "How to Build a Solar-Powered Water Purifier." For Dummies, March 26, 2016. https://www.dummies.com/article/home-auto-hobbies/garden-green-living/sustainability/green-building/how-to-build-a-solar-powered-water-purifier-194406/.

Demillo Wagner, Gina. 2021. "'Can I Eat That?' Answer the Question With the Universal Edibility Test." *Backpacker* (blog), November 30, 2021. https://www.backpacker.com/skills/universal-edibility-test/.

Deziel, Chris. 2024. "What to Know About Home Wind Turbines." *Family Handyman* (blog), March 22, 2024. https://www.familyhandyman.com/article/home-wind-turbines/.

Dine-A-Chook. 2023. "How to Build a $20 Chicken Coop." Dine-A-Chook, February 2, 2023. https://www.dineachook.com.au/blog/how-to-build-a-20-chicken-coop/.

DIY $50 EMERGENCY WATER FILTER, 2023. https://www.youtube.com/watch?v=lGw0AVV5Hek.

DrinkPrime. 2023. "How to Check If Your Drinking Water Is Safe to Drink?," August 14, 2023. https://drinkprime.in/blog/drinking-water-is-safe-to-drink/.

Earthquake Country Alliance. 2017. "Home." Earthquake Country Alliance, January 25, 2017. https://www.earthquakecountry.org/.

Emergency Essentials. 2017. "8 Simple DIY Emergency Shelters for Conquering the Great Outdoors." Be Prepared, July 11, 2017. https://www.beprepared.com/blogs/articles/8-simple-diy-emergency-shelters-conquering-great-outdoors.

———. 2014. "10 Natural Remedies That Work." Be Prepared, April 25, 2014. https://www.beprepared.com/blogs/articles/10-natural-remedies-that-work.

Emergency Prep Gear, n.d. "The Best Survival Cordage, Paracord, Line, Rope." https://www.emergencyprepgear.com/survival-cordage.

Energy Saver, n.d. "Planning for Home Renewable Energy Systems." Energy.gov. Accessed November 15, 2024. https://www.energy.gov/energysaver/planning-home-renewable-energy-systems.

Energy Saving Trust, n.d. "Biomass." Energy Saving Trust. Accessed November 15, 2024. https://energysavingtrust.org.uk/advice/biomass/.

Eureka! 2015. "6 Ways to Start a Fire Without Matches or a Lighter -," October 6, 2015. https://eurekacamping.johnsonoutdoors.com/us/blog/6-ways-start-fire-without-matches-or-lighter.

FEMA. 2021. "Shelter In Place Guidance," November 2021. https://www.fema.gov/sites/default/files/documents/fema_shelter-in-place_guidance.pdf.

Frankel, Miriam, and Matt Warren. 2023. "How Hunger Can Warp Our Minds." BBC, August 22, 2023. https://www.bbc.com/future/article/20230822-how-hunger-can-warp-our-minds.

Gardener's Supply. 2024. "Guide to Raised Beds: Plans, Timing, Tending |." www.gardeners.com, March 21, 2024. https://www.gardeners.com/how-to/raised-bed-basics/8565.html.

Gemeš, Nikola. 2024. "How to Easily Build Your Own DIY Composting Toilet." GreenCitizen, March 20, 2024. https://greencitizen.com/blog/diy-composting-toilet/.

Gordon, Brad. 2023. "15 Common Residential Uses of Solar Power in Your Houses." 604-GO-SOLAR, October 2, 2023. https://www.604gosolar.com/15-common-residential-uses-of-solar-power-in-your-homes/.

Hamilton. 2023. "The 8 Types of Home Water Filters And Filtration Systems," August 23, 2023. https://www.callhamilton.com/blog/the-8-types-of-home-water-filters-and-filtration-systems.

Haupt, Angela, and Claire Young. 2022. "How to Prepare for 8 Types of Disasters." EverydayHealth.com. https://www.everydayhealth.com/healthy-home/what-to-do-when-disaster-strikes.aspx.

Hepler, Linda. 2018. "How to Stop Bleeding: From Cuts, Wounds, and More," September 17, 2018. https://www.healthline.com/health/first-aid/stopping-bleeding#bleeding-emergencies.

Higgins, Doug, and Kristin Krokowski. 2012. "Using Crop Rotation in Home Vegetable Garden." Wisconsin Horticulture, April 9, 2012. https://hort.extension.wisc.edu/articles/using-crop-rotation-home-vegetable-garden-0/.

HomeBiogas. 2024. "How To Make Biogas at Home – A Step-by-Step Guide," February 21, 2024. https://www.homebiogas.com/blog/how-to-make-biogas-at-home/?srsltid=AfmBOooCQvpLEbZFCbpko38STNV3cbSdelVDPf9jeDE-stI07eG6l1Kf.

———. 2024. "What Is Biogas? A Beginners Guide," February 9, 2024. https://www.homebiogas.com/blog/what-is-biogas-a-beginners-guide/.

How to Build a Two-Bucket Water Purification System to Prepare for a Disaster. 2021. YouTube Video. Cedar Hills Ready! Disaster Prep. https://www.youtube.com/watch?v=XLyOd_2tFV0&t=151s&ab_channel=CedarHillsReady%21DisasterPrep.

Innovative Water Solutions LLC. 2024. "Rainwater Harvesting 101 | Your How-To Collect Rainwater Guide," October 18, 2024. https://www.watercache.com/education/rainwater-harvesting-101.

Jackson, Kenzie. 2023. "Crafting a Survival Garden In Your Backyard - Greenhouse," October 30, 2023. https://growingspaces.com/survival-garden/.

James, Leslie. 2020. "5 Ways to Signal for Help in the Wilderness." OutThere Colorado, December 29, 2020. https://denvergazette.com/outtherecolorado/multimedia/5-ways-to-signal-for-help-in-the-wilderness/collection_64700178-e9b5-53e6-9615-c9e599841260.html.

(JHM), Johns Hopkins Medicine, n.d. "Burns and Wounds." Accessed November 19, 2024. https://www.hopkinsmedicine.org/health/conditions-and-diseases/burns.

Johnson, Jon. 2024. "How Long Can You Live without Water? Facts and Effects." Medical News Today, July 9, 2024. https://www.medicalnewstoday.com/articles/325174.

Joque, Jim, and Susan Wowk. 2022. "Compass and Map Reading 101: Basics for the Beginner." Snowshoe Magazine, April 19, 2022. https://www.snowshoemag.com/compass-and-map-reading-101-basics/.

Judd, Angela. 2022. "Garden Troubleshooting Guide: How to Identify & Solve Common Garden Problems." *Growing In The Garden* (blog), January 7, 2022. https://growinginthegarden.com/garden-troubleshooting-guide-how-to-identify-solve-common-garden-problems/.

Katella, Kathy. 2022. "How To Be More Resilient: 8 Strategies for Difficult Times." Yale Medicine, May 31, 2022. https://www.yalemedicine.org/news/resilience-strategies-pandemic.

Keith, Patrick. 2020. "Guide to Smoking Meat," November 9, 2020. https://www.off-gridlivingnews.com/blog/guide-to-smoking-meat.

Kennedy, John F. 1962. *1962 State of the Union*. Washington D.C.

Klemm, Sarah. 2024. "4 Keys to Strength Building and Muscle Mass." Eat Right: Academy of Nutrition and Dietetics, May 10, 2024. https://www.eatright.org/fitness/physical-activity/benefits-of-exercise/4-keys-to-strength-building-and-muscle-mass.

Lamp'l, Joe. 2018. "Raised Bed Garden from A - Z | What to Know | Joe Gardener®." *Joe Gardener® | Organic Gardening Like a Pro* (blog), March 8, 2018. https://joegardener.com/podcast/raised-bed-gardening-pt-1/.

Laws, Joe, and Andrea Chymiy. 2018. "Physical Fitness for Preppers." The Prepared, May 25, 2018. https://theprepared.com/prepping-basics/guides/survival-fitness/.

Lee, Jeanne. 2024. "How to Live Below Your Means Without Feeling Deprived." Nerd-Wallet, July 10, 2024. https://www.nerdwallet.com/article/finance/live-below-your-means-without-feeling-deprived.

Lobermeier, Kayla. 2022. "Complete Guide: How to Raise, Butcher, and Process Chickens." Under A Tin Roof, August 2022. https://underatinroof.com/blog/2022/8/22/how-to-butcher-and-process-chickens.

Louv, Matt. 2023. "12 Edible Bugs That Could Help You Survive." *Backpacker* (blog), October 25, 2023. https://www.backpacker.com/survival/12-edible-bugs-that-could-help-you-survive/.

LS Fire Group. 2021. "How to Put out Different Types of Fires | Pyrotec." Pyrotec Fire Protection Ltd, March 1, 2021. https://www.pyrotec.co.uk/news/how-to-put-out-different-types-of-fires/.

Mack, Eric. 2024. "My Best Tips After Setting Up My Own Off-Grid Solar Energy System." CNET, April 22, 2024. https://www.cnet.com/home/energy-and-utilities/my-best-tips-after-setting-up-my-own-off-grid-solar-system/.

MacWelch, Tim. 2019. "A Guide to the 15 Best Survival Traps of All Time." Outdoor Life, October 21, 2019. https://www.outdoorlife.com/how-build-trap-15-best-survival-traps/.

———. 2019. "Survival Shelters: 15 Best Designs and How to Build Them." Outdoor Life, October 16, 2019. https://www.outdoorlife.com/survival-shelters-15-best-designs-wilderness-shelters/.

Magyar, Cheryl. 2023. "10 Animals To Raise For Self-Sufficiency." *Rural Sprout* (blog), July 7, 2023. https://www.ruralsprout.com/raise-animals-for-self-sufficiency/.

Malinoski, Pam. 2018. "How To Use Companion Planting Strategies To Maximize Your Home Garden Yield." Farmers' Almanac - Plan Your Day. Grow Your Life., April 25, 2018. https://www.farmersalmanac.com/companion-planting-guide.

Mawer, Rudy. 2024. "15 Proven Tips to Sleep Better at Night." Healthline, May 29, 2024. https://www.healthline.com/nutrition/17-tips-to-sleep-better.

McEntire, Katie, and Alina Bradford. 2024. "What Should I Do in the Event of a House Fire?" SafeWise, October 2, 2024. https://www.safewise.com/home-security-faq/house-fire/.

McKay, Brett, and Katie McKay. 2021. "9 Ways to Start a Fire Without Matches." *The Art of Manliness* (blog), May 16, 2021. https://www.artofmanliness.com/skills/outdoor-survival/9-ways-to-start-a-fire-without-matches/.

———. 2021. "Surviving in the Wild: 19 Common Edible Plants." *The Art of Manliness* (blog), June 1, 2021. https://www.artofmanliness.com/skills/outdoor-survival/surviving-in-the-wild-19-common-edible-plants/.

Mileham, Alex. 2022. "Tinder Fire Starter: Best Examples." *Survival Courses Tasmania* (blog), December 6, 2022. https://survivalcoursestasmania.au/tinder-fire-starter/.

Montana, Angela. 2015. "Five Shelter-Building Mistakes to AVOID in a Survival Situation." Blog. Montana Outdoor, May 25, 2015. https://www.montanaoutdoor.com/2015/05/five-shelter-building-mistakes-to-avoid-in-a-survival-situation/.

Mount Sinai. n.d. "Poisoning First Aid," https://www.mountsinai.org/health-library/injury/poisoning-first-aid.

myenergi. 2022. "Renewable Energy Facts: 10 Truths| Myenergi IE ," August 12, 2022. https://www.myenergi.com/ie/guides/renewable-energy-facts-10-truths-that-will-amaze-you/.

National Agricultural Library, n.d. "Humane Methods of Slaughter Act | National Agricultural Library." Accessed November 14, 2024. https://www.nal.usda.gov/animal-health-and-welfare/humane-methods-slaughter-act.

National Grid Group. 2023. "What Is Biogas?," February 23, 2023. https://www.nationalgrid.com/stories/energy-explained/what-is-biogas.

National Oceanic and Atmospheric Administration, n.d. "U.S. Wind Climatology |." National Centers for Environmental Information (NCEI). Accessed November 15, 2024. https://www.ncei.noaa.gov/access/monitoring/wind/.

Nemett, Adam. 2021. "How to Build Raised Garden Beds | Thunderbird Disco Homestead

- Permaculture Homesteading Blog." Thunderbird Disco Homestead.https://www. thunderbirddisco.com/blog/how-to-build-raised-garden-beds.

Nicolaides, Paulo. 2021. "15 Ways to Store Food without Electricity - Self Sufficient Homesteading." *Self Sufficient Homesteading* (blog), March 6, 2021. https://www.self-sufficienthomesteading.com/self-sufficiency/ways-to-store-food-without-electricity/,___ https://www.selfsufficienthomesteading.com/self-sufficiency/ways-to-store-food-without-electricity/.

Nielsen, Lorin. 2020. "20 Best Crops for A Survival Garden." Epic Gardening, March 23, 2020. https://www.epicgardening.com/survival-garden/.

NOAA National Severe Storms Laboratory, n.d. "Flood Basics." Text. Accessed October 22, 2024. https://www.nssl.noaa.gov/education/svrwx101/floods/.

———, n.d. "Winter Weather Basics." NOAA National Severe Storms Laboratory. Accessed   October   22,   2024. https://www.nssl.noaa.gov/education/svrwx101/winter/.

Nolan, Tara. 2021. "Preparing Raised Beds for Winter: Essential Autumn To-Dos." Savvy Gardening, November 1, 2021. https://savvygardening.com/preparing-raised-beds-for-winter/.

(NPS), U.S. National Park Service, n.d. "Two Ways to Purify Water (U.S. National Park Service)." Accessed November 1, 2024. https://www.nps.gov/articles/2wayspurify-water.htm.

(NSRDB), National Solar Radiation Database. n.d. "NSRD." https://nsrdb.nrel.gov/.

Off Grid Dwellings. 2023. "6 Vegetables For Your Survival Garden - Garden Off The Grid Living," December 12, 2023. https://offgriddwellings.com/6-vegetables-for-your-survival-garden-garden-off-the-grid-living.

Off-grid Collective, n.d. "Off-Grid Hydropower." Accessed November 15, 2024. https://www.offgridcollective.co.nz/pages/off-grid-hydropower.

Oklahoma Department of Emergency Management. 2024. "Toolkit: 12 Ways to Prepare: Practice Emergency Drills." Oklahoma Department of Emergency Management. https://oklahoma.gov/oem/news/newsroom/12-ways-to-prepare--practice-emergency-drills-.html.

Olivadese, Marianna, and Maria Luisa Dindo. 2023. "Edible Insects: A Historical and Cultural Perspective on Entomophagy with a Focus on Western Societies." *Insects* 14, no. 8 (August 4, 2023): 690. https://doi.org/10.3390/insects14080690.

(OLLU), Our Lady of the Lake University, n.d. "Shelter in Place Tips,." https://www.ollusa.edu/campus-safety/emergency-preparedness/shelter-in-place-tips.html.

Overlooked Survival Item You Need to Learn to Make, 2023. https://www.youtube.com/watch?v=tsEdO-lmnkA.

Palethorpe, Stephen. 2019. "DIY: Solar Dehydrator -." Renew, March 3, 2019. https://renew.org.au/renew-magazine/diy/diy-solar-dehydrator/.

Peterson, Bahtya. 2024. "10 Home Security Tips For The Off-Grid." *Home Safeguard Pro* (blog), March 4, 2024. https://homesafeguardpro.com/10-home-security-tips-for-the-off-grid/.

Positive Adventures. 2020. "How to Build an Emergency Shelter (PLUS... How a Single

Tarp Could Save Your Life!).” Blog, May 2020. https://www.positiveadventures.com/blog/emergency-shelter.

PROINSO, n.d. “DIY Off-Grid Solar System.” *PROINSO - Award-Winning for Solar Energy Projects* (blog). Accessed November 15, 2024. https://www.proinso.net/blogs/build-diy-off-grid-solar-system/.

Rea, Debbie. 2021. “Tips for Using Rain Barrels.” *The Gardener Wife* (blog), November 2, 2021. https://thegardenerwife.com/2021/11/02/tips-for-using-rain-barrels/.

Ready. 2023. “Biohazard Exposure | Ready.Gov.” https://www.ready.gov/biohazard.

———. 2022. “Cybersecurity | Ready.Gov.” https://www.ready.gov/cybersecurity.

———. 2024. “Earthquakes | Ready.Gov.” https://www.ready.gov/earthquakes.

———. 2024. “Hurricanes | Ready.Gov.” https://www.ready.gov/hurricanes.

———. 2024. “Landslides & Debris Flow | Ready.Gov.” https://www.ready.gov/landslides-debris-flow.

———. 2023. “Pandemics | Ready.Gov.” https://www.ready.gov/pandemic.

Robinson, Lawrence, Jeanne Segal, and Melinda Smith. 2018. “How to Start Exercising and Stick to It.” HelpGuide.org, November 2, 2018. https://www.helpguide.org/wellness/fitness/how-to-start-exercising-and-stick-to-it.

Ruiz, Chris. 2013. “Top 10 Multi Use Survival Tools for Your Bug Out Bag.” *The Bug Out Bag Guide* (blog), November 27, 2013. https://www.thebugoutbagguide.com/multi-purpose-survival-tools/.

Sakawsky, Anna. 2019. “Homemade Rain Barrel DIY Project - The House & Homestead,” April 14, 2019. https://thehouseandhomestead.com/homemade-rain-barrel/.

———. 2017. “Pickling 101: The Ultimate Guide to Everything Pickled.” *The House & Homestead* (blog), June 28, 2017. https://thehouseandhomestead.com/ultimate-guide-to-pickling/.

Semeco, Arlene. 2023. “How to Start Exercising: A Beginner’s Guide to Working Out.” Healthline, February 1, 2023. https://www.healthline.com/nutrition/how-to-start-exercising.

Seymour, John. 2023. “Start a 1-Acre Homestead: Layout Planning – Mother Earth News,” April 27, 2023. https://www.motherearthnews.com/homesteading-and-livestock/self-sufficient-homestead-zm0z11zkon/.

Solar Learning Center, n.d. “How Does Solar Power Work on a House? Your Questions Answered Archives.” *Solar.Com* (blog). Accessed November 15, 2024. https://www.solar.com/learn/how-do-solar-panels-work/.

Spahr, Jason, and Arianne Spahr. 2023. “Planning a Garden Layout.” SurvivalGardenSeeds, January 10, 2023. https://survivalgardenseeds.com/blogs/survival-garden-training/planning-a-garden-layout.

Statista. 2023. “Rainiest States in the U.S. 2023.” Statista. https://www.statista.com/statistics/1101518/annual-precipitation-by-us-state/.

Survival Jack. 2023. “Homestead Animal Husbandry: 10 Tips for Raising Healthy Livestock,” September 27, 2023. https://survivaljack.com/2023/09/homestead-animal-husbandry-10-tips-for-raising-healthy-livestock/.

Svalbarði, n.d. “How Long Can You Live Without Water? Facts And Effects To Survive.” Svalbarði Polar Iceberg Water. https://svalbardi.com/blogs/water/living-without.

Tampa Bay Regional Planning Council. 2020. "Evacuate or Stay?" https://townofreding-tonshores.com/wp-content/uploads/2020/06/evacuate-or-stay.pdf.

Tarver, Ben. 2020. "How Much Does the Average Roof Replacement Cost." B&M Roofing | Commercial & Residential Roofing in Colorado, December 17, 2020. https://bmroof-ing.com/how-much-does-the-average-roof-replacement-cost/.

Team New Terra, n.d. "Planning a Survival Garden." Accessed November 6, 2024. https://www.new-terra-natural-food.com/planning-a-survival-garden.html.

Traister, Lee. 2024. "How to Butcher a Rabbit." Lady Lee's Home, March 20, 2024. https://ladyleeshome.com/how-to-butcher-a-rabbit/.

Truchon, Jeff. 2023. "Survival Shelters — Which Type Is Right for You?" The Atomic Bear, January 6, 2023. https://www.theatomicbear.com/blogs/news/survival-shel-ters-which-type-is-right-for-you.

UC Davis Health. 2022 "How to Spot a Concussion and What to Do If You Suspect a Brain Injury." Cultivating Health, September 14, 2022. https://health.ucdavis.e-du/blog/cultivating-health/how-to-spot-a-concussion-and-what-to-do-if-you-suspect-a-brain-injury/2022/09.

(URMC), University of Rochester Medical Center, n.d. "A Guide to Common Medicinal Herbs - Health Encyclopedia - University of Rochester Medical Center." Accessed November 19, 2024. https://www.urmc.rochester.edu/encyclopedia/content.aspx?contenttypeid=1&contentid=1169.

U.S. Department of Agriculture, n.d. "Humane Methods of Slaughter Act | National Agri-cultural Library." https://www.nal.usda.gov/animal-health-and-welfare/humane-methods-slaughter-act.

US Department of Commerce, NOAA, n.d. "Understand Tornado Alerts." NOAA's National Weather Service. Accessed October 24, 2024. https://www.weather.-gov/safety/tornado-ww.

———, n.d. "What to Do During a Tornado." National Weather Service. NOAA's National Weather Service. Accessed October 24, 2024. https://www.weather.-gov/safety/tornado-during.

U.S. Fire Administration, n.d. "Home Fire Escape Plans." U.S. Fire Administration. Accessed October 23, 2024. https://www.usfa.fema.gov/prevention/home-fires/pre-pare-for-fire/home-fire-escape-plans/.

Vaccaro, Adam. 2024. "Home Wind Turbines: Overview, Products, and Costs." Energy-Sage, July 11, 2024. https://www.energysage.com/about-clean-energy/wind/small-wind-turbines-overview/.

Van Sloun, Nancy. 2015. "Natural Remedies for Everyday Illnesses." Allina Health, November 28, 2015. https://www.allinahealth.org/healthysetgo/heal/natural-reme-dies-for-everyday-illnesses.

Veterans Off-Grid. 2020. "The Benefits of Using Renewable Energy in Your Home," March 31, 2020. https://www.veteransoffgrid.org/articles-were-reading/the-bene-fits-of-using-renewable-energy-in-your-home.

Waddington, Elizabeth. 2024. "Self Sufficient Farming And Living - A Guide To Planning And Planting | Polytunnel Gardening," May 10, 2024. https://blog.firsttunnels.-co.uk/self-sufficient-farming/.

Walden University, n.d. "Why Emergency Preparedness Matters." Accessed October 23, 2024. https://www.waldenu.edu/online-masters-programs/ms-in-criminal-justice/resource/why-emergency-preparedness-matters.

Water Boy. 2020. "How to Know If Your Water Is Safe to Drink | Water Boy," November 11, 2020. https://waterboyinc.com/blog/how-to-know-if-your-water-is-safe-to-drink.

Wateroam. 2024. "A Guide to Rural Rainwater Harvesting and Filtering for Southeast Asia." WATEROAM, September 4, 2024. http://www.wateroam.com/32/post/2024/04/a-guide-to-rural-rainwater-harvesting-and-filtering-for-southeast-asia.html.

WebstaurantStore. 2024. "How to Cure Meat," August 7, 2024. https://www.webstaurantstore.com/article/258/how-to-cure-meat.html.

Wondersmith. 2023. "Foraging 101: How to Get Started (plus Some of My Favorite Resources)." Blog. The Wondersmith, February 18, 2023. https://misswondersmith.com/blog/2019/introtoforaging.

Yost, John, n.d. "Survival Hunting and Trapping | Yost Survival Skills | Bushcraft and Outdoor Skills." *Survival Skills and Bushcraft for the Modern Survivalist* (blog).https://yostsurvivalskills.com/survival-hunting-trapping/.

www.ingramcontent.com/pod-product-compliance
Lightning Source LLC
Chambersburg PA
CBHW071520120626
46550CB00006B/2295